# The Tourist's Guide to Hong Kong, with short trips to the Mainland of China. [With plans, etc.]

R. C. Hurley

*The Tourist's Guide to Hong Kong, with short trips to the Mainland of China. [With plans, etc.]*
Hurley, R. C.
British Library, Historical Print Editions
British Library
1897
94 p. ; 8°.
10058.ccc.26.

## The BiblioLife Network

This project was made possible in part by the BiblioLife Network (BLN), a project aimed at addressing some of the huge challenges facing book preservationists around the world. The BLN includes libraries, library networks, archives, subject matter experts, online communities and library service providers. We believe every book ever published should be available as a high-quality print reproduction; printed on- demand anywhere in the world. This insures the ongoing accessibility of the content and helps generate sustainable revenue for the libraries and organizations that work to preserve these important materials.

The following book is in the "public domain" and represents an authentic reproduction of the text as printed by the original publisher. While we have attempted to accurately maintain the integrity of the original work, there are sometimes problems with the original book or micro-film from which the books were digitized. This can result in minor errors in reproduction. Possible imperfections include missing and blurred pages, poor pictures, markings and other reproduction issues beyond our control. Because this work is culturally important, we have made it available as part of our commitment to protecting, preserving, and promoting the world's literature.

## GUIDE TO FOLD-OUTS, MAPS and OVERSIZED IMAGES

In an online database, page images do not need to conform to the size restrictions found in a printed book. When converting these images back into a printed bound book, the page sizes are standardized in ways that maintain the detail of the original. For large images, such as fold-out maps, the original page image is split into two or more pages.

Guidelines used to determine the split of oversize pages:

• Some images are split vertically; large images require vertical and horizontal splits.
• For horizontal splits, the content is split left to right.
• For vertical splits, the content is split from top to bottom.
• For both vertical and horizontal splits, the image is processed from top left to bottom right.

TOURIST GUIDE
TO
HONG KONG

AND MAINLAND

BY R.C. HURLEY

# ADVICE TO TOURISTS.

>-·-<

Get rid of the idea that you can possibly see anything
Hongkong by strolling about the lower levels. A fortnight or more
be most delightfully spent in doing this Island thoroughly.

In no place in the whole world are thére so many beautiful sp
so much varied scenery, or such lovely sea views,—yet travellers p
through in increasing numbers yearly and not one out of a hundred
those who so travel know anything of the place beyond its few curio sh

Buy a Guide Book and a map of the Island. Put up at on
the Hill District Hotels where you will be well housed and fed;—
early and walk or take a chair round and round this gem of the Far
along its numerous hill roads, and say if you have ever seen anything
compare with it in all your life anywhere.

You will live in an absolutely pure atmosphere during your
and tram-cars will bring you into town in about ten minutes at any t

## TIME TABLE.

### WEEK DAYS.

7.30 a.m. to 10.30 a.m............Every quarter of an ho
11.30 a.m. to 12.30 p.m...........Every half hour.
12.30 p.m. to 2.30 p.m............Every quarter of an ho
3.30 p.m. to 8.00 p.m............Every quarter of an hou
Night cars at 8.45 p.m. and 9 p.m. and from 9.45 p.
to 11.15 p.m. every half hour.

### SATURDAYS.

Extra Night cars at 11.30 and 11.45 p.m.

### SUNDAYS.

10.30 a.m. and 10.40 a.m.

Noon to 2 p.m. ....................Every quarter of an hou
3 p.m. to 9 p.m. ....................Every quarter of an hou
Night cars from 9 p.m. to 11 p.m., every half hour.

THE HONGKONG HIGH-LEVEL TRAMWAYS COMPANY, LIMITED

*Office: 38 & 40, Queen's Road Central, Hongkong.*

THE MOUNT AUSTEN HOTEL

Since purchased by the Military for use as a Sanitarium.

# HONGKONG, CANTON AND MACAO STEAM-BOAT
## Company, Limited
### AND
# CHINA NAVIGATION CO., LD.

## STEAMERS:

| | | | |
|---|---|---|---|
| FATSHAN | 2260 TONS | HONAM | 2363 TONS |
| HANKOW | 3073 ,, | POWAN | 2338 ,, |
| HEUNGSHAN | 1998 ,, | WHITE CLOUD | 798 ,, |

## Particulars of Sailings.

**To Canton.**—Every morning except Sunday, at 8, and every evening, except Saturday, at 5.30 in Winter and 6 p.m. in Summer, returning, two departures daily from Canton, Sunday excepted.

**To Macao,**—Each weekday about 2 p.m. returning, leaves Macao the following day at 7.30 a.m.

**From Macao to Canton.**—Every Monday, Wednesday and Friday at 7.30 a.m.

**From Canton to Macao.**—Every Tuesday, Thursday and Saturday at 8 a.m.

*The above times of departure will be adhered to as strictly as possible, but are occasionally subject to slight deviation to suit tides, &c.*

## FARES:

To CANTON ........................................$5 each way.
,, MACAO.............................................$3 ,,
,, or from CANTON and MACAO ...........$3 ,,
Meals (including Table wine) $1.50 each.

*Further particulars may be obtained at the office of the Company,*

18, Bank Buildings, Queen's Road Central.

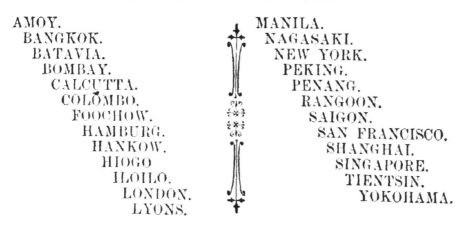

# Peninsular & Oriental Steam Navigation Co.

The steamers of this Company leave Hongkong with THE ENGLISH MAIL every alternate Thursday conveying passengers and cargo to

## Singapore, Penang, Colombo, Australasia, India, Aden, Port Said, Ismailia, Mediterranean Ports, Plymouth, and London.

## EXTRA STEAMERS

RUN TO THE

### Straits Ports, Colombo, Port Said, Marseilles and London

*at intervals of about a fortnight. These Steamers have excellent accommodation for a limited number of passengers.*

Fortnightly departures to SHANGHAI by Mail steamers and by Extra steamers at frequent intervals.

To YOKOHAMA *via* Nagasaki and Kobe *passing through the Inland Sea,* departures every fortnight.

Particulars regarding dates of sailing, Rates of Passage Money, Freight, &c. may be obtained on application at the Offices of the Company—

### PRAYA CENTRAL, HONGKONG.

# KRUSE & CO.

Queen's Road     HONGKONG.     Connaught House

WHOLESALE & RETAIL TOBACCONISTS.

## BEST BRANDS of MANILA CIGARS.

*Genuine Havana Cigars.*

## EGYPTIAN CIGARETTES.

# SMOKING TOBACCO.

Views of Hongkong and Canton.

# Indo-China Steam Navigation

## COMPANY, LIMITED.

—∘∘✖∘∘—

## RATES OF PASSAGE:

*BY STEAMERS DIRECT TO*

## PENANG, SINGAPORE, AND CALCUTTA.

### FIRST CLASS.

| CALCUTTA to HONGKONG. | | HONGKONG to CALCUTTA. | |
|---|---|---|---|
| To Penang,......Rs. 135. | Return,......Rs. 220. | To Singapore,......$ 50. | Return,.........$ 80. |
| To Singapore ...Rs. 150. | Return,......Rs. 240. | To Penang,.........$ 65. | Return,.........$105. |
| To Hongkong,...Rs. 250. | Return,......Rs. 425. | To Calcutta, ......$125. | Return,.........$225. |

The Company's Steamers also connect at Hongkong with the Coast ports, Swatow, Amoy and Foochow, and with the Northern Service to Shanghai, Yangtze river ports, Chefoo, Taku, and Tientsin for Peking and Mongolia.

*N.B.*—Return Tickets available either by INDO-CHINA Co.'s or APCAR & Co.'s Steamers.

# Apcar Line of Steamers.

## RATES OF PASSAGE.

### BY STEAMERS DIRECT TO

## PENANG, SINGAPORE, AND HONGKONG

### FIRST CLASS

| CALCUTTA TO HONGKONG. | HONGKONG TO CALCUTTA. |
|---|---|
| To Penang,......Rs. 135. Return,......Rs. 220. | To Singapore,......$ 50. Return,.........$ 80. |
| To Singapore,...Rs. 150. Return,......Rs. 240. | To Penang,.........$ 65. Return,.........$105. |
| To Hongkong,..Rs. 250. Return,......Rs. 425. | To Calcutta, ......$125. Return,.........$225. |

### SECOND CLASS

| CALCUTTA TO HONGKONG. | HONGKONG TO CALCUTTA. |
|---|---|
| To Penang,....Rs. 100. Return,....Rs. 150. | To Singapore,....$ 35. Return,......$ 56. |
| To Singapore,...Rs. 110. Return,....Rs. 175. | To Penang,......$ 45. Return,......$ 75. |
| To Hongkong,..Rs. 200. Return,....Rs. 320. | To Calcutta, ....$ 80. Return,......$130. |

Children travelling with their parents are charged as follows :— One child under three free ; if more than one child, every additional child ¼ fare. If over three and up to ten years, ½ fare. European maid servants travelling with ladies and children and occupying a berth in first class cabin, at two-thirds of first class fare. Native servants with diet, to Penang, Rs. 23-8 ; Singapore, Rs. 29-8 ; Hongkong, Rs. 44. Native servants, without diet, at deck rates.

### Native Deck Passengers, without diet :—

| PENANG. | SINGAPORE. | HONGKONG. |
|---|---|---|
| Rs 20. | Rs 25. | Rs 35. |

## APCAR & Co.,

*Owners, Steamers—*

| | |
|---|---|
| "ARRATOON APCAR,"..................2,200 tons. | |
| "LIGHTNING," .........................3,306 „ | |
| "CATHERINE APCAR," ...............2,715 „ | |

*N.B.*—Return Tickets available either by APCAR & Co.'s or INDO-CHINA Co.'s Strs.

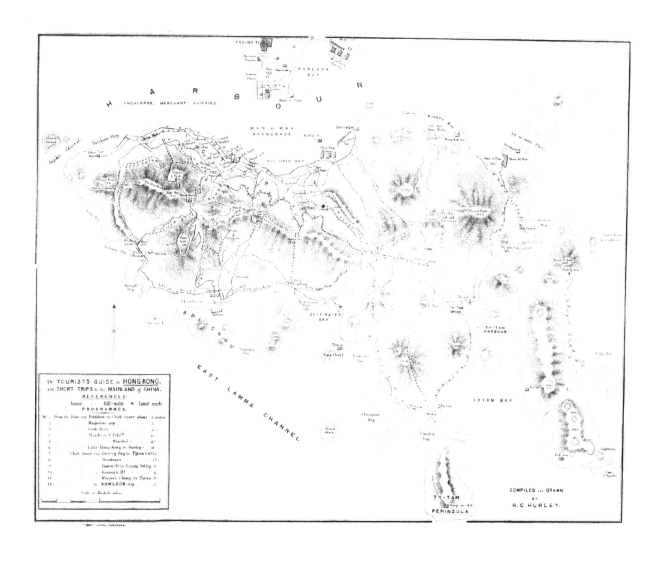

The TOURISTS GUIDE to HONG KONG,
with SHORT TRIPS to the MAINLAND of CHINA.

REFERENCES:

PROGRAMMES.

COMPILED and DRAWN
BY
R. C. HURLEY.

# CHINA MERCHANTS STEAM-NAVIGATION Co.

*STEAMER SERVICES BETWEEN ALL THE TREATY PORTS.*

## Hongkong, Canton and Shanghai.

S.S. "FUSHUN."       S.S. "KWANGLEE."

*Weekly Sailings.*

## Shanghai, Chefoo, Tientsin & Newchwang.

S.S. "HAE AN."       S.S. "HSIU FUNG."
S.S. "SHIN YU."       S.S. "FUNG SHUN."
S.S. "POO CHI."       S.S. "HSIN CHI."
S.S. "HAE TING."

*Bi-Weekly Sailings.*

## Shanghai & Foochow.    Shanghai & Ningpo.

S.S. "HAE SHIN."       S.S. "KIANG TIEN."

*Bi-Weekly Sailings.*      *Alternate daily Sailings.*

## Shanghai & Wenchow.

S.S. "POO CHI."

## Shanghai, Amoy, Sawtow, Hongkong & Canton.

S.S. "CHI YUEN."       S.S. "TOO NAN."
S.S. "YUNG CHING."       S.S. "KUNG PING."
S.S. "IRENE."       S.S. "MEE FOO."
S.S. "CHIN TUNG."       S.S. "LEE YUEN."

*Bi-Weekly Sailings.*

## Canton & Macao.    Hankow & Ichang.

S.S. "KIANG TUNG."    S.S. "KULING."    S.S. "KWEI LEE."

*Daily Sailing.*      *Weekly Sailings.*

*FIRST CLASS ACCOMMODATION AND EXCELLENT CUISINE.*

For further particulars, apply at the Company's Offices :

Head Office: - - - 1, Foochow Road, Shanghai.

Branch  ,,    - - - { Praya West, Hongkong,
{ Canal Road, Canton.

# DOUGLAS STEAM-SHIP Co., Limited.

## ❋ STEAMERS ❋

| | |
|---|---|
| "HAITAN." | "HAIMUN." |
| "FORMOSA." | "NAMOA." |
| "HAILOONG." | "THALES." |

These favourite steamers have regular sailings between

## HONGKONG, SWATOW, AMOY, FOOCHOW, TAMSUI & TAIWANFOO.

To SWATOW *and* AMOY *three times per week.*

„ FOOCHOW, *weekly.*

„ TAMSUI, *twice per week.*

„ TAIWANFOO, *every fortnight.*

Through Tickets granted to Shanghai *via* Coast ports.

## EXCELLENT PASSENGER ACCOMMODATION.

For further particulars as to Freight, Passage, &c.

Apply to

## DOUGLAS, LAPRAIK & Co.,
*General Managers.*

# United States Mail Lines.

| Pacific Mail Steamship Company. | Occidental & Oriental S.S. Co. |
|---|---|

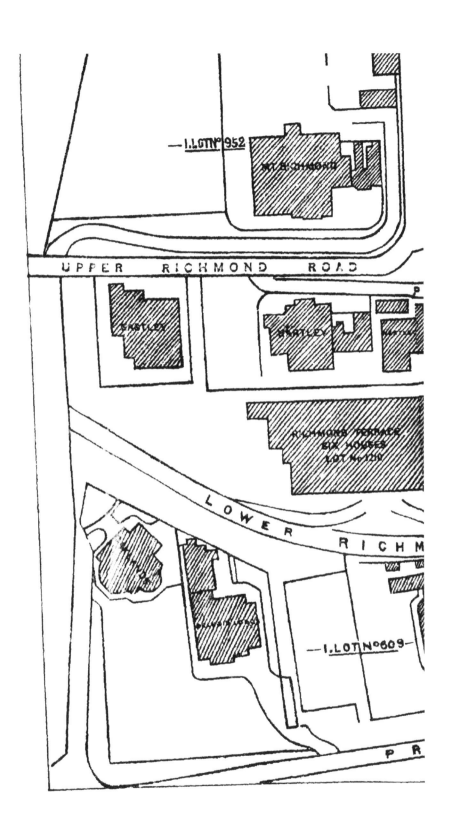

# RICHMOND TERRACE ESTATE

— SKETCH PLAN OF PROPERTY —

— SCALE 100 FEET TO 1 INCH —

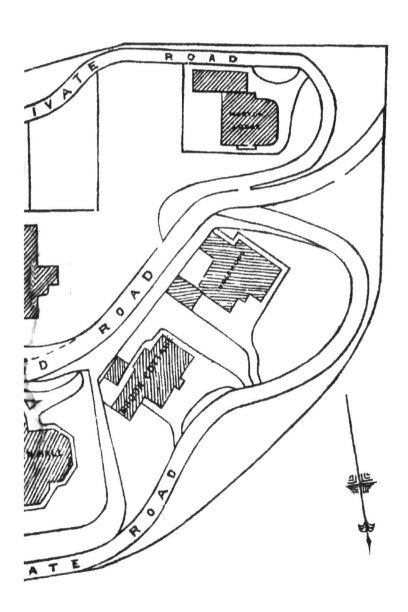

KOWLOON ESTATE

The Officers Mess—Hong Kong Regiment, with Recreation Ground fronting onto the Sea Shore—Kowloon Bay.

VIEW ON THE RICHMOND ESTATE FROM THE EAST.

To the left of the picture is "Mount Richmond" the residence of the Governing Director and to the right three of the recently built residences
Oaklands, Beloon Lodge, and Eden Hall, with Richmond Terrace between

KOWLOON ESTATE

The Native Officers Quarters of the Hong Kong Regiment with the Durbar and Mosque to the left.

KOWLOON ESTATE

The Officers Mess—Hong Kong Regiment, with Recreation Ground fronting onto the Sea Shore—Kowloon Bay.

# THE
# TOURISTS' GUIDE

TO

# HONGKONG

WITH

## SHORT TRIPS

TO THE

# *Mainland of China*

BY

R. C. HURLEY.

HONGKONG:
PUBLISHED BY R. C. HURLEY, 12 & 13, BEACONSFIELD ARCADE.
PRINTED BY THE "HONGKONG PRINTING PRESS," D'AGUILAR STREET,
1897.

TO THE LATE

## Mr. John D. Humphreys.

IN ADMIRATION OF THAT ENTERPRISING SPIRIT, THAT CLOSE
APPLICATION AND ENERGY, AND THAT INDOMITABLE
PLUCK WHICH HAS ALWAYS CHARACTERISED
THE MANY SUCCESSFUL UNDERTAKINGS
WITH WHICH HIS NAME HAS BEEN
MOST PROMINENTLY ASSOCIATED
IN THE

### FAR EAST:

AND

IN APPRECIATION
OF THAT READY, YET THOUGHTFUL
KINDNESS AND GOOD NATURE, WHEN AND
WHEREVER OPPORTUNITY HAS OCCURRED FOR DISCREETLY
EXERCISING THE SAME,

THIS BOOKLET IS

## Inscribed

BY THE AUTHOR.

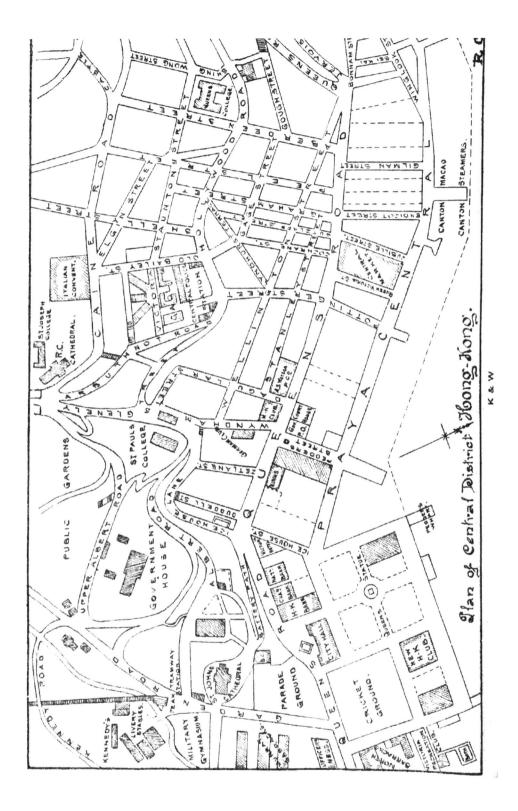

Plan of Central District Hoong-Kong.

# RATES FOR HIRING, &c.

## Limits (Victoria) Mount Davis **W.** to Causeway Bay **E.**

### Chairs, 2 COOLIES—inside limits :

½ hour, 10 cents.     1 hour, 20 cents.     3 hours, 50 cents.

6 hours, 70 cents.     Day, 6 to 6, $1.00.

### Chairs, 4 COLLIES—beyond limits.

1 hour, 60 cents.     3 hours, $1.00.     6 hours, $1.50.     Day, 6 to 6, $2.00.

### JINRICKSHAS.

¼ hour, 5 cents.     ½ hour, 10 cents.     1 hour, 15 cents.

Every subsequent hour, 10 cents.

*It is a wise precaution to take the number of the chair or ricksha when hiring.*

## Hongkong High Level Tramway Co.,
### *LIMITED.*

## TIME TABLE.

### WEEK DAYS.

7.30 A.M. to 10.30 A.M. every quarter of an hour.

11.30 A.M. to 12.30 P.M. every half hour.

12.30 P.M. to 2.30 P.M. every quarter of an hour.

3.30 P.M. to 8.00 P.M. every quarter of an hour.

NIGHT CARS at 8.45 P.M. and 9 P.M. and from 9.45 P.M. to 11.45 P.M. every half hour.

### SATURDAYS.

EXTRA NIGHT CARS at 11.30 P.M to 11.45 P.M.

### SUNDAYS.

8.45 A.M. to 10.15 A.M. every half hour.
10.30 A.M. and 10.40 A.M.

Noon to 2 P.M. every quarter of an hour.

3 P.M. to 8 P.M. every quarter of an hour.

IGHT CARS 8.45 P.M. and 9 P.M. and from 9.45 P.M. to 11.15 P.M. every half hour.

*SPECIAL CARS, by arrangement at the Company's Office, 38 & 40, Queen's Road Central.*

## FRENCH MAIL.

Leaves 11 A.M., alternate WEDNESDAYS.

## ENGLISH MAIL.

Leaves 11 A.M., alternate THURSDAYS.

## HONGKONG & KOWLOON FERRY,

### TIME TABLE.

### DAY SERVICE.

*A Launch will leave ICE-HOUSE STREET WHARF and the KOWLOON GODOWN WHARF every quarter of an hour, from 6 a.m. to 7.45 p.m.*

### NIGHT SERVICE.

| Leave Kowloon Godown Wharf. | Leave Ice-House Street Wharf. |
|---|---|
| 8.15 P.M. | 8.00 P.M. |
| 8.45 ,, | 8.30 ,, |
| 9.15 ,, | 9.00 ,, |
| 9.45 ,, | 9.30 ,, |
| 10.45 ,, | 10.00 ,, |
| 11.45 ,, | 11.00 ,, |
|  | Midnight. |

# LIST OF ILLUSTRATIONS.

## MAPS, &c.

# PREFACE.

*The general object* of this book is to promote the many varied interests of the residents and visitors, and, in such attempt, to contribute also as much information as possible necessary to the well being and enjoyment of the tourist during his sojourn in the Colony.

According to report this want has long been felt. Information in a readable form that will interest without causing fatigue, furnishing at the same time data sufficiently reliable to satisfy where only a limited period for personal investigation is available.

It is a regretable fact, that in recent years so many have passed through Hongkong without ever setting foot on shore, so to speak; or at any rate without seeing anything of the place beyond the Hotel, the Clock Tower and the few curio shops in Queen's Road. Why should this be so— ?

Hongkong is, by a great way, the most important centre in the Far East and although it cannot boast of any special features of natural wonderment, yet as an European Colony of 55 years growth, having germinated on the soiless surface of a barren rock, it is indeed a wonderful specimen of Anglo Saxon pluck and energy of which every Briton may well be proud ; and one, from which, by a careful study of its history (Europe in China Dr. E. J. EITEL, P.D.) many a sound object lesson may be profitably learned.

The mainland to the North, none the less interesting from its close proximity, also furnishes special additional features. There, are to be found, opportunities of seeing various phases of Chinese life in China amongst the more simple agricultural and fishing industries with their curious but ingeneous primitive methods.

Again, who shall say but what some day, sooner or later, this very spot may not provide the theatre for a grand performance of some of the most thrilling acts in the Great Drama of the Far East. Its relative position at least points out the most natural direction in which Britian in China should first expand her immediate sphere of influence, and, therefore, something of its topography and general condition may also be of passing interest to the average visitor.

The Historical sketch, Chronological Record of Events; traversing as it does, a period of nearly three centuries, has been compiled with the greatest care and from the most reliable sources; and, the Author, whilst trusting that his book will amply fulfil the object for which it is ostensibly written, further presumes to hope that it may find its way to many friends at home, wherever that happy place may be, and prove of lasting interest and value to those who, from various causes, are not permitted the opportunity of seeing and experiencing for themselves.

HONGKONG, March, 1897.

# INTRODUTION.

## THE ISLAND OF HONGKONG.

*The first impression* of the visitor, on approaching the island from the South as he views its many peaks and ridges from the deck of the Steamer, is that of a pleasant but mild excitement combined with feelings of contentment and security,—for he is probably aware that Hongkong is the most prominent Outpost of Western Civilization, Commerce and Shipping in the Far East,— is a British Crown Colony—and a Free Port.

As the finer details of the picture improve with the Mount Austin Hotel and the numerous pretty residences in the summit levels, the pine clad slopes, the Douglas Castle and the Sanitorium of the French Fathers, on the ridge below, pleasant anticipation approaches almost to a fascination and there naturally follows a longing to explore these peaceful hill districts.

To assist in accomplishing this very natural desire, a series of easy programmes and a carefully compiled chart of the island with a complete road plan, having many special routes marked in red and the fullest descriptive particulars necessary—are here furnished.

In no part of the Far East is there so much to repay the lover of grand natural scenery in comparative miniature, both in landscape and seascape, from the simple picturesque to the sublime, as will be seen in this beautiful Island Home. Here, will also be found, representatives of many races, many peoples, one and all in the full and equal enjoyment of that perfect freedom, that true liberty, which for centuries has been the birthright of those, regardless of colour or creed, who elect to reside under the protection of the Union Jack.

Again, of pleasing interest to the casual visitor and especially to the amateur botanist, a collection of over sixty specimens in variety of the fern species can readily be gathered from the sides of the mountain roads and in the numerous small water courses which will be seen in every direction.

For the Amateur photographer subjects are endless; whether it be the magnificent mountain views, the varieties of the marine, or the oddities of native life and character—all are at his disposal with the least possible effort.

Nor should the Curio-shop be forgotten, as the Antiquarian with the assistance of the *Astute* Celestial will soon discover. Everything that is produced in any part of this vast Empire is procurable here in Hongkong, convenient for selecting, packing and shipping under one's own supervision.

For transport, mails and telegraphy ; direct communication with all parts of the civilized world is at once possible, these facilities alone contributing to enhance the merits of the place.

Add to all this the advantage of a complete change of climate within the short space of ten minutes—from the Queen's Road to the Peak by tramway—with its corresponding constitutional benefits, and, an abundant supply of pure filtered water.—Who shall dare say that Hongkong is not deserving of a full share of the Tourists' Time and Patronage—?

# HISTORICAL.

## 1625 to 1896.

———◆◇◆———

Hongkong is a British Crown Colony. Its inhabitants comprise some 7,000 British and Europeans including the garrison, 250,000 Chinese and 4,000 Portuguese.

The voluntary cession of the island of Hongkong to the British in 1841 forms a sequence to the events recorded in the history of the tradal and other relations with the Empire of China extending over a period of more than two centuries.

It was in 1625 that the East India Company, at that time the most powerful maritime trading corporation in the world, sought to extend their sphere of operations beyond the confines of the East Indies to the Far East. With this object in view, experimental agencies were first started at Tai Wan on the West coast of the Island of Formosa and also at Amoy across the channel close to the mainland.

These two ventures, owing to the good fortune of having met with a kindly welcome by the local government officials, under the then reigning Ming Dynasty, proved fairly encouraging, and, two years later a further advance was made through the Portuguese settlement Macao, in the direction of Canton. This effort, however, was not attended with marked success. The Portuguese, very naturally, could not appreciate the presence of such a powerful rival as a participant in what they alone had so far developed and kept to themselves.

A few years later, however, in 1634 another venture in the direction of Canton was started, this time with better prospects, as the East India Company had been able to arrange over the head of the Macao Authorities, with the Governor of Goa, Portuguese India ; and as a result the British ship " London " on arriving at Macao, was graciously received by the authorities. Subsequently the " London " proceeded up to Canton where by a friendly Viceroy she was granted full permission to trade at that port.

Ten years later, in 1644, the Ming Dynasty had been overthrown giving place to the present Ta-Tsing (Great pure) Dynasty, and, following this important event, what had promised to develop into a very friendly and lucrative commercial intercourse was for a time to be completely blighted and undone.

From the experience already gained, and the incentive thereby created, the commencement of British trade with the Southern Capital may be said to date from about this period ; although, through various causes of one kind and another it did not properly flourish until Oliver Cromwell had concluded a treaty with Portugal on a basis of International equality and reciprocity whereby the ships of both nations should enjoy free access to any part of the Far East.

The sudden change in the reigning dynasty of the Empire caused a complete reversal of the previously promising prospects of Western enterprise. The East India Company had begun to contemplate a bright future for their, so far, experimental efforts ; but, although boastfully successful in controlling and managing so many of the Eastern Potentates, the Celestial of the Far East, especially the New Tartar Species, proved to be an altogether unknown quantity.

Quite a new experience,—the Officials from the highest to the lowest, even in the ordinary preliminaries of introduction, first demanded a complete submission amounting almost to an abject humiliation, before even condescending to receive.

Before foreign vessels could approach their ports or enter any of their rivers, it was beholden on the captains of such vessels to petition in the most servile manner for a permit, and then to wait for an indefinite time the pleasure of some subordinate for the result.

Passing on to 1681 the East India Company's Agencies at Amoy and Tai Wan were closed, had been in fact destroyed, and their ships were now all consigned to Macao. In 1685 the Amoy Agency was re-established.

Things now remained in a passive state for a period of nearly 15 years when in 1699 fresh efforts were made to open up negociations with the Chinese Government by the appointment of a Minister and Consul for the whole Empire.

This, a Royal Commission, was simply ignored by the arrogant Celestials and a merchant (Emperor's Merchant) was appointed by the high officials to supervise—having the full authority to conduct any and every class of negociation that might possibly occur.

The new arrangement was, as the only alternative, accepted by the Europeans and trade continued to develop but very slowly, as might have been expected under such trying circumstances. In the year 1715 things became fairly settled, all ships proceeding to Macao, and sending their agents up to Canton to arrange the best terms they could for entering the port and discharging their cargoes. Five years later, the authorities at Peking, to enable them better to check the

revenue collected through the medium of this foreign
trade, levied a duty of 4 per cent. *ad valorum* on all
imports and exports, and the Emperor's Merchant was
superseded by the Co-Hong, a Company of Merchants,
who were individually and severally responsible both
to the foreign traders and to the government. In 1725
a further fixed tariff was arranged also to protect the
revenue which it failed to do, owing to the Chinese
ancient system of "squeeze" which differs somewhat
from our more regular methods. In 1727 another
special tax of 10 per cent was levied on both imports
and exports, but in the following year, on the accession
of the Emperor Kien Lung it was done away with. At
this period of history Canton was annually visited by
some eight vessels ; 4 British, 2 French, 1 Danish and
1 Swedish.

Many years of quiet now ensued until in 1754 a
new order of things obtained, the Co-Hong became
monopolists being allowed to control the whole of the
foreign trade which henceforth was to be confined to
the port of Canton alone. The Amoy Agency on account
of some smuggling irregularities, was in trouble, and
as a consequence the East India Company's representatives sought to make special arrangement for the trade
of that port, but owing to the underhand dealings and
influence of the Canton Officials, they did not succeed.

With affairs in such a state the only chance left
was to submit matters to Peking. This was done, and
an Imperial Commission was appointed to investigate,
with the result that the Chief Commissioner was bribed
by the Canton Officials, and the supplicant representatives of the East India Company were brutally treated
whilst actually inside the Yamen of the Viceroy : their
interpreter was imprisoned and $1,250 demanded for
his release.

Another period of patience and long suffering until in 1771 permission was finally granted to Europeans to reside at Canton during the winter months, as the ships generally arrived in the fall season and left again late in the spring.

This change of residence proved very convenient and speedily brought about the dissolution of the Co-Hong system.

Ten years later another monopolist trading society sprung up, the 13 Mandarins, really the old Co-Hong under a new name.

This society enjoyed the privilege of having the entire control of the Foreign trade, was under the direct supervision of the officials, and possessed, through their aid, a guarantee fund raised by a special tax.

To this new system the East India Company and others once more graciously submitted and it appears to have worked smoothly for nearly twenty-five years, as not until 1805 was there any further interference, when another special tax was levied for the purpose of providing the cost of coast defences against foreign ships, which of late had considerably increased their armaments in proportion to the increased value of their cargos.

A few years later another difficulty which promised to develop into something very serious was destined to disturb the Commercial equilibrium. The officials finding that the balance of trade so far in their favour, imports against exports, was gradually decreasing, made a rule in the year 1818 considerably restricting the export of bullion (silver) which rule, in its application, greatly harassed the operations of the foreign Merchants.

It was about this time that the tea trade went ahead by leaps and bounds and some six years later the first shipments were made to Australia direct.

In 1831 trouble again arose owing to the still increasing outflow of silver and additional restrictions were imposed which threatened the suspension of trade entirely ; finally, however, the demands were once more acceded to. In this case the Chinese felt assured that they had gained an unmistakable victory, but at the same time they could scarcely understand, and were not a little perplexed at the very noticeable change which had come over the demeanor of the East India Company's representatives as well as all the other foreign merchants.

In the following year, 1832, so marked had been the effect of this noticeable change, the reserved yet independent tone of the foreigners, that the bonds were considerably loosened in the direction of free trade, and as a consequence no less than 74 British ships entered at the port of Canton within the twelve months.

Two years later a very disturbed feeling was evident amongst the high Officials, who, constantly making every effort in their power to regain their now fast failing supremacy, seemed to be greatly distressed at the serious turn things were taking, War clouds were faintly visible in the distance, and they had not the least conception of what that meant.

About this time the East India Company's monopoly ceased, trade with China was thrown open, and by the arrival of representatives from the Home Government as Superintendents, preparations of a permanent character appeared to be under way.

Amongst other institutions a Court of Justice was established having jurisdiction over all British subjects both on land and on the high seas within 100 miles of the Coast. Later on in the year Lord Napier and suite arrived as chief representative of the Home Government to be assisted by two representatives of the East India Company's service. At an early date Lord Napier repaired to Canton with a full staff, Captain Elliott, R.N. as Master Attendant, to pay his official visit to the Viceroy. Here he met with an extremely rude reception, his servants and baggage being very roughly handled. It was reported in native quarters that some "foreign devils" had come. Lord Napier submitted patiently handing in his credentials from his King, which credentials were insolently rejected because they were not properly inscribed with the character of petition 禀 (*pien*) This state of affairs following so closely on the troubles caused by the late financial friction promised soon to develop into something much more serious. However, after a little delay some of the officials were deputed to interview Lord Napier for the purpose of ascertaining what he really wanted. And upon the refusal of Lord Napier to adopt the humiliating style of petition demanded; China still persisting in her claims to supremacy over all foreign barbarians, he was told that he must leave the City forthwith. To hasten his departure orders were issued by the officials to the effect that all intercourse with British Merchants should cease; trade was suspended, native servants were prohibited from continuing service, the provision supply was stopped and the shipment of cargo by any British vessel was forbidden.

A further effort of a very serious character was also attempted ; this was, persuading British Merchants not to submit to or acknowledge the authority of the Lord Napier Expedition, but to accept that of the Local Officials through the Hong Merchants as heretofore.

When it was seen that the disaffection of British subjects against the special representative of their sovereign was impossible, further determined efforts were made to starve them out, all the establishments being surrounded by soldiers as a sort of menace to the British merchants.

Finally, as if through a sudden collapse of their
brazen temerity, the Merchants were informed by the
Officials that they might leave Canton via Whampoa for
Macao but were never to return. "You know" said a
mandarin to an English Merchant "We have cut off the
"trade with the English ; there is to be no more inter-
"course, our great Emperor's orders have been proclaimed
"and all beneath the heavens have but to tremble and
"obey ; this is self evident. What to us their buttons
"and musical boxes, their knives with six blades cork-
"screw and file. All these will find no more market in
"the flowery land.

The outlook on all sides was now becoming so
serious that Lord Napier considered it advisable to
order two frigates to come up to Whampoa. This was
done, and on their arrival, companies of marines were
landed and soon succeeded in reaching the quarter where
the Europeans were located. On this very simple show
of force the Chinese Officials at once climbed down, re-
commending negociations through the Hong Merchants
and offering to resume trade immediately if the two
frigates should leave the river and Lord Napier retire
to Macao. This very peaceful solution was forthwith
arranged ; the frigates left the river and Lord Napier
in a sad state of health, owing to the trying ordeal
through which he had passed, proceeded in a native
boat to Macao. The trip occupied five days, whereas
the distance should have been covered in twenty-four
hours. This tedious delay told very unfavorably on
Lord Napier's health and he died a fortnight after his
arrival in the Holy City.

As may be imagined, following on what has just
been related, the political atmosphere, locally, was
very much overcharged with feelings akin to a volcano

immediately preceding eruption. But, the time had not come yet.

The Opium question was just beginning to add fuel to the then inwardly raging fire, and although the traffic, as reported upon by Sir George Best Robinson and his colleagues, was very objectionable, no steps were taken to diminish it. Sir George was no advocate of the trade and applied for permission to prevent British ships from engaging in it but without any satisfactory result. The Chinese still persisted in not recognising any British Authority, and consequently a period of quiescent policy followed for the next eighteen months with a very unpromising outlook for the future.

After all these long years of patience and perseverence, incessant vexation and suffering, it had suddenly begun to dawn upon some of the leading merchants that an altogether different line of policy might improve matters. It was said, and wisely said, that "nothing can be done with a threat." A paragraph which appeared in the local paper "The Canton Register" April 25th, 1836, stated. "If the Lion's paw is to be put down on any part of the south side of China let it be Hongkong,— guarantee it a free port, and, in less than ten years, it will be the most important mart east of the Cape." From this time a complete change of attitute, superceding all previous policy, both to the Portuguese at Macao as well as to the Chinese Authorities, became evident. At Canton, International Equality was the demand of the day. The Hong-merchants were ignored and all official communications were made direct. The struggle was nearly at an end. China's stubborn assertion of supremacy over all the outside nations was rapidly becoming a myth before England's quiet but persistent claim for International Equality.

Fortunately at this time, as if to strengthen the position taken up, H. M. Ships "Volage" and "Hyacinth" happened to be anchored in the river; and, supported by this show of force, a letter was sent to the highest local official, Commissioner Lin, the Officer down from Peking to investigate affairs; demanding that a proclamation be issued withdrawing all the threats and obnoxious orders which had been given, to the danger of the British Merchants, their trade and their property; pending negociations from England for the peaceful adjustment of all the difficulties.

Commissioner Lin was at the Bogue on a tour of inspection, and the letter was duly sent from H. M. S. "Volage," by Mr. Morrison, an intepreter, to await a reply, which reply was to be returned by a boat flying a white flag. Nothing satisfactory came of this communication but, a squadron of Chinese war-junks, 29 sail, was seen to be shifting position and slowly making towards H. M. Ships. Things were looking serious. H. M. Ships were immediately got under way and prepared to engage. The Chinese war-junks then cautiously anchored in close order and returned the letter sent to Commissioner Lin the previous day, without any answer. This was quite sufficient for the British Commanders. Within three-quarters of an hour all that was left of the 29 sail retired in great confusion, 3 having been sunk, 1 blown up, and the others with their crews in a sorry plight, more or less seriously damaged.

This was the first lesson in International jurisprudence, manners and common courtesy; and I may say the first introduction to the principal factor in the scientific civilizing power of the age, given to the haughty Chinese Officials. What they thought of, or how they appreciated it remains to be told.

The following amusing account circulated in Canton with a picture representing a fighting and a fireship, with descriptions, will perhaps convey some idea of the impression the British ships, even of that date, made upon the child-like Celestial.

" Their length is more than three hundred feet,
Their height and breadth more than thirty feet,
They use iron guns of great size and strenght,
Having the look of being covered with iron garments.
The fire-ship has wheels on both sides
Which are made to revolve of fire made of coal.
She runs with the swiftness of a fleet horse,
While sails made of white cloth cover her masts above and
She heeds neither a fair wind nor a contrary wind,      [below
At her prow she carries the figure of the Demon of des-
On all sides are seen rows of cannon,                      [truction
Truly the figures of these vessels cause one to shudder."

Captain Elliott, having taken over all responsibility now became a very prominent character. His task, with its many existing complications, added to which were the impending difficulties in managing the new peculiarities of the Celestial temperament, was any thing but an easy one. For two centuries this temperament had been literally spoiled; nursed, cosseted and petted, all its whims and fancies studied, loaded with any quantity of presents, and actually flattered,—by admission through a passive submission,—that it represented the Supreme Power of the Universe.

The Opium difficulty was to be the final signal for the commencement of a war-like demonstration, and intimidation in various ways was adopted by the Chinese to attain their defensive ends.

Annoyance to the British Merchants in every possible manner continued to be the daily study of the Officials from the highest to the lowest.

Happily at this critical moment with the outlook at its blackest, there was a faint rift visible in the fast gathering storm clouds.

From what had been lately doing in the British Parliament it was more than surmised that preparations were at last afoot, and that an expedition would soon start for the scene of all these Far Eastern troubles.

This was happily confirmed when in June, 1840, a fleet began to arrive comprising 17 men-of-war and 27 troop ships; bringing 3 regiments, a corps of engineers, a corps of sappers and miners, in all 4,000 men under the command of Sir J. J. Gordon Bremer. Besides these there was a contingent from the East India Company, 4 of their armed steamers fully equipped.

The Chinese on becoming aware of the approach of this expedition, simply said, "What can they do if we quietly wait on the defensive and watch their movements."

Of course a dead lock had followed on the first lesson administered, already referred to. $5,000 was offered for the head of Captain Elliott, with various smaller sums ranging as low as $500 for the heads of any of the other officers, and the merchant and shipping communities were in a state of great consternation.

In reality the climax had at last arrived. British trade was entirely suspended. British patience was almost exhausted,—and British pluck was ripe for the fray. On the 4th June, 1840, notice was given of the blockade of the Canton River and about the same time the island of Chusan, at the mouth of the Yangtsze, was also occupied.

The stated object of this programme was to obtain, —reparation for insults and injuries of the past, the opening of at least 5 Treaty ports to foreign Commerce, with sundry other conditions of minor importance.

In the following January, Captain-Elliott, finding himself no nearer a peaceful settlement, determined to bring matters to a crisis ; so an ultimatum was sent to Kislien, then Viceroy of Chihli, who had been appointed Imperial Commissioner to investigate the cause of, and pacify these barbarian disturbances, giving 24 hours' notice for compliance with the demands made,—But, before going further, I must relate an amusing anecdote, told by Captain Eyres of H.M.S. "Modeste." "One evening at dusk, a small China boat was reported pulling for the ship. It was allowed to come alongside, when a Chinaman, getting on deck asked to see ' Miss-ee' Kaptan, who appeared, but as the visitor preferred to see him alone Eyres let him down into the cabin. He carefully locked the door and quickly made known the object of his visit, which was, that inasmuch as Eyres and he were not enemies he saw no reason, in fact considered it madness, for them to *shoot* at one another! ' My show you. My long you No. 1 *good flen*, what for fightee ? Large Man-la-le makee fightee, he please ; s'pose to-molla hav got fightee, you no puttee plum you gun, my no puttee plum my gun ; puttee fire physic (powder) can do velly well, makee plenty noise, makee plenty smoke,—my no spilum you, you no spilum my!' A short time after, all the forts having been destroyed as Captain Eyres watched the bombardment, who should he see amongst the first to take to the open, with his tail tied round his head, but his. ' No 1 good flen ! ' running as if the devil himself was after him, Another Chinaman, a boat man, who happened to be on the firing side seized his skull to move off, yelling with all his might, 'my *chin-chin* you, stop *littee*, my go odder sy ? During the attack on Canton, an old-china street porcelain merchant, named Cum-Chong, told us that as he was crossing the river in a passage-boat with many others, a round shot tore through it killing several and wounding many, when, as he said. 'My puttee head insi holo' the chances being against another shot coming through the same place.

But, for all their ignorance of the art of war the Chinese believed themselves invincible, for said they : 'Think of the Hoo-mun' (the Bogue) ' what monuments of skill! The sight of these frowning battaries causes the bravest to shrink, and when the terrible engines, they contain are opened, the remotest corners of the world are agitated with the shock. They are, moreover, defended by men who have proved invincible in innumerable conflicts'. And, notwithstanding the havoc which our fleet made of their defences, still the barbarians were considered as beaten, and their own imaginary prowess describled thus when the city was ransomed :—

" How detestable are these *rebellious* demons !
They have *confused* the people, pillaged their houses
But the *gods*, did they not cause to descend terrific rain?
The villagers came forward in their wrath,
The drums were beaten, the strong and valiant dealt
　slaughter.
Fortunate indeed was it, for soon the enemy was annihilated.
The blessings of great peace are now restored, and all
　may return to their avocations without molestation."

The notice having expired and no answer forthcoming, the bombardment of the Bogue-forts commenced at 9.30 on January 7th 1841. In less than half an hour some 18 war-junks were destroyed, the forts captured by assault, with 500 killed and 300 wounded. By 11 o'clock in the forenoon the action was over, the British flag flying above the ruins of the supposed invulnerable Bogue and the Chinese braves scattered in heavy retreat.

Thus ended the second lesson, of the right of might and the physical power of Western Civilization. When China set up her wall of exclusion and seclusion, somewhat as *our Cousins* across the Pacific are doing to-day, she forgot to mount cannon upon its ramparts. China is a self contained country embracing every climate and every food and, as with all countries similarly placed, the soil becomes very fertile in the abnormal developement of conceit. Her cry was the cry of Diojenes "Stand out of *my* Sunlight. She was not aware of the fact, that Commercial intercourse, conducted upon the highest principles of integrity, represents the healthiest flow of the life blood of our very existance. Let us not, however, take unction to ourselves for these inglorious contests. "War! cried Captain Sherard Osborn, God save the mark. Let not our countrymen run away with the idea that I or any other naval or military man look upon a war in China as war in its legitimate sense, a field where personal honour and glory are to be had. No, believe me! few who have shared in our operations in China fancy any such thing."

In the issue of these hostilities, amongst other settlements the island of Hongkong was now offered in cession to Great Britain by Kishen on behalf of the Chinese Government.

It was accepted, and on January 25th 1841, Sir E. Belcher with some of his officers landed at 8.15 just below the hill in the centre of the present City of Victoria, now occupied by the Chinese as a recreation ground, and considering themselves the first British possessors, drank to Her Majesty's health with "Three Cheers."

On the following day when the whole squadron arrived in the harbour, possession was formally taken by

Commodore Bremer in the name of Queen Victoria. The true position was also fixed by Sir E. Belcher as being 22° 16′ 30″ North Latitude—114° 06′ 30″ East Longitude.

This performance was as unexpected as it was sudden.—

The population of the Island at the time of its formal occupation by the British counted some 2,000 souls; respresenting three distinct families,—the Puntis or aborigines, the Hakkas or strangers from the highlands of the interior, and the Hoklos, a sturdier type of men hailing from the Coast-ports to the north.

These people were mostly engaged in farming, wood cutting and fishing after a sort of primitive arcadian fashion, but in a very short space of time this was to be all changed for the navy, the stonemason and the bricklayer, besides the carrying coolie, whose part in the progress of the immediate future was to be no unimportant one: the population consequently increased at an extraordinary rate.

All that was now necessary was Peace,—which Plenty would naturally follow.

It was scarcely to be expected that this second lesson, with its greatly humiliating effect on the Celestial, would be at one forgotten, regardless of the great show of sincerity made by the Imperial Commissioner Kishen in the very prominent part which he had played; but so it happened that on the 20th July, 1841, the very day when Sir J. J. Gordon Bremer formally took possession of the new colony, Kishen received an Imperial Edict from Peking that once more completely changed the aspect of everything from peace to war.

Whilst the British fleet had remained in full force outside the entrance to the Tientsin river an apparently genuine show of sincerity amongst the officials inside was on parade. But, directly the fleet had left, the mask was raised, and sincerity was supplanted by a determined effort for vengeance. Orders were issued to at once exterminate the barbarians. Kishen was to have a chance of retrieving his lost prestige by successfully executing these orders, and a war of extermination was to begin immediately. Fortunately the British had remained in a thoroughly prepared state, with Captain Elliott in full command, therefore little time was wasted and on the 18th February the Chinese fired the first shot.

The following day the British fleet commenced once more to rendezvous in the Canton River. War was declared a few days later, and by public proclamation throughout the district, Captain Elliott's head was wanted for $50,000. Movements were rapid. Under cover of the darkness a landing was effected to the south of the Bogue well out of range of the Chinese fire, a battery was erected by the British soldiers and at dawn the Chinese positions were shelled and carried. So sharp had been the conflict that within a couple of hours, most of the guns were spiked, 1,000 prisoners taken in the forts with 352 killed and wounded. The prisoners after being compelled to bury the dead were told to return to their homes.

Early next day another position further up the river, garrisoned by 2,000 picked men and mounting 100 guns was, after a hard fight, also taken. An old British ship which the Chinese had converted into a frigate was captured and destroyed, and, as the fleet moving slowly in the direction of Canton subdued one position after another, so the merchantmen closely followed until Whampoa was reached when trade was at once resumed on March 1st, 1841.

The British war-ships were now almost within range of the city, and the Acting Prefect had applied for a 3 days' truce, which was granted; but as nothing came of it, Captain Elliott secured to himself a strong position under the southern wall and anchored, assuming there might possibly be some further opposition.

When the British men-of-war were within sight the curiosity of the poor people was something extraordinary. The roofs of the houses, and the streets on the river-side, were crowded and otherwise thronged with Chinese seeking for a look at the strange monsters, and, representations of them, with the sailors in various grotesque and impossible attitudes, were cut on blocks of wood, and innumerable copies struck off and sold about the city and suburbs for less than a half-penny. On the topgallant yard-arm could be seen a barbarian in the foreign dress of the last century standing unconcernedly without support of any kind looking through a spyglass. The hulls of the sailing vessels were laughable enough, great guns on wheels being the most conspicuous objects. Men were scattered about in the queerest of attitudes, and flags and streamers were streaming out in every direction, regardless of the wind. The steamers were supplied with enormous wheels everywhere; astern, under the bows, and in duplicate on the sides.

On March 4th, 1841 a proclamation was issued stating, that the Emperor's bad advisers were responsible for this serious trouble, that the war was against the Chinese Government and not against the inhabitants, who were exhorted to resume trade peaceably.

In spite of the excitement, now that the port had been forced open, business flourished; while the Officials, who seemed still bent on their war of extermination had all along been secretly making preparations in the south west quarter of the City for the renewal of hostilities.

On the British commanders discovering this, they at once proceeded to the work of destruction, which was the only way to bring these Officials to their senses. Seven batteries mounting 105 guns were forthwith destroyed as well as a fort in the Macao passage about 3 miles to the south of Canton. For a few days nothing further was done, time being allowed for overtures towards a settlement, until on March 10th. the Chinese fired on a flag of truce; thereupon the work of destruction was resumed, this time close up to the city where a big fleet of war-junks lying at anchor was soon demolished. The place was now completely at the mercy of the British and patience was further extended to admit of another attempt being made to arrive at a peaceful understanding, this time not altogether without its reward.

For the second time the City was spared without a ransom on condition that the show of hostile preparations should be discontinued and trade resumed. Ultimately a convention was concluded with a special Commissioner and everything now seemed to be progressing satisfactorily. However, all this time the officials were, in an underhand way, still urging on the inhabitants to prosecute the war of extermination. Money, all of which was spent in munitions of war, was forthcoming from the business that was daily put through.

New cannon were cast and placed in position, masked batteries were constructed along the river banks and any number of war-junks and fire-ships were got ready for the attack. Now, although everything on the surface appeared to be so peaceful, a very careful watch was being kept, and well founded rumours of

what was really going on, prompted Captain Elliott to
postpone the departure of the fleet, which, by this time
ought to have left for the North. He was patiently
waiting for the Chinese to open the ball when *he* would
provide the orchestra. But, as it was noticed that the
battery on Shameen to the West of the City, facing the
river and covering the Macao passage, was, although
destroyed, only 2 months previously, about to be recon-
structed and armed, he peremptorily called a halt,
demanding the immediate suspension of the work ; and,
as no proper heed was given to his demand, preparations were forthwith made for the worst. Re-inforce-
ments were at once ordered up from Hongkong.

The Chinese were now doing their utmost to keep
up the show of friendship, in the expectation of being
able to deceive Captain Elliott, although they were
at the same time quietly massing troops inside the City
walls. As another blind, a proclamation was now issued
to the inhabitants who were showing signs of uneasiness,
urging them to remain quiet and to continue trading
with the foreigners without any fear or suspicion.

Strange to say throughout all this crafty performance
their must have been a lot of party-jealousy at Official
Head-quarters, as one of these gentlemen had taken it
upon himself secretly to organize a night attack, by
means of fire-ships, on the British position.

As luck would have it information of this plot was
forthcoming in time, and Captain Elliott, issued a
circular March 21st, 1841, calling upon all foreigners to
leave the city before sunset. Towards midnight the
attack commenced, a number of fire-boats, their crews
being armed with long boarding pikes and carrying fire
balls and stink-pots drifted with the tide in the
direction of the British ships. The moment the first of

these boats appeared it was fired upon, when in reply, all the forts and masked batteries at once opened fire and the Chinese soldiery proceeded to ransack the establishments of the absentees. As the British were fortunately well prepared, this night attack signally failed, and little or no damage was done except to the property of the merchants. Next morning the work of distruction was actively resumed. Everything having the appearance of a battery was invested and reduced, and over 100 war junks and fire-ships were captured and burned. Preparations were now made for an attack on the city, so on the 24th May after the usual salute in honour of Her Majesty's Birthday, the transport of troops through shallow water to the different stations appointed, commenced.

Proceeding up a branch of the river in the direction of the West gate, a landing was effected and a start made about 9 o'clock on May 25th. The four outlying forts were attcked and captured at the point of the bayonet, and a camp under cover of the guns on the wall was also dispersed.

While all this was going on a counter move on the southern side of the city was being made, and the ships from the river were bombarding the Tartar General's Yamen. This triple event quite upset the calculations of the Chinese Officials who were prepared only in those quarters where attack never came. They were demoralized, and a panic raged in the city when it was discovered that the big guns on the city wall could not be trained to do any service. The next day rain fell incessantly which completely stopped further operations. This was fortunate, as the British were now short of guns and ammunition, however all was ready and in perfect order again before sundown. On the following morning, at the moment when the bugle was to sound the attack, news came that a Treaty of Peace had been concluded between Captain Elliott and Yick Shan and Ki King. This, the Treaty of Canton, was based on the following stipulations

The Chinese soldiers, some 35,000 of them, were to evacuate the city without any display of banners. The Imperial Commissioners were to leave the city within six days and to proceed to a distance of at least sixty miles.

That the following payments being made within one week, $6,000,000 as a ranson for the City and $335,000 for damage done to individual property, &c., the British troops and ships should retire beyond the Bogue. Further, a promise was to be given not to resume any hostile preparations, but to open Whampoa and Canton to trade immediately.

The indemnity for the cost of the war was to be left for settlement between the two Governments direct.

Thus ended the third lesson, and now, surely enough had been done by way of instructing these people as to the proper respect due to outside barbarians. This ten days fighting had certainly placed matters on a very different footing, had brought the campaign to a termination, and had set the British troops free just as the hot season was approaching.

Five months later, approbation was expressed by Her Majesty the Queen of what had been done, but Captain Elliott got neither credit nor thanks.

*All honour is due to the memory of brave Captain Elliott, who served his country nobly, obtaining more from China than any other representative nation. The Island of Hongkong and $6,335,000.*

The new diminutive baby colony, experiencing no end of trials and troubles at the period of its birth, was nevertheless, with its parent and protector 10,000 miles away, a wonderful progeny ; a startling surprise to the world. Some believed in it and others did not, hence the usual sufferings of infancy promised to be rather severe upon it.

The Chinese fiscal authorities of the district to which it had recently belonged could not understand the change. Taxes which for generations had been collected from the farmers and fishermen on the island, had no longer to be paid : equally surprised were the farmers and the fishermen. However, beyond the disturbing effects which might naturally be looked for, consequent on the administration of the third lesson to the Canton authorities, already described, there was little to interfere with the immediate growth of the place. The population, which prior to the occupation numbered about 2,000, had within a few months increased to 5,600 and with such a fountain-head as the Chinese Empire, gave untold promise for the future.

On the 15th May Sir Henry Pottinger was selected to fill the position of sole Plenipotentiary and Minister Extraordinary to China. Arriving at Macao, August 10th he at once notified the Canton Officials that the slightest infringement of the terms of the truce would lead to the immediate renewal of hostilities.

At this sudden and unexpected warning, the literati and gentry viewed the attitude of superiority as a studied insult and an unbearable disgrace. These gentry had never known what it was to submit to any such dictatorial message. What! they cried, shall we who rule the world, be dictated to by outside barbarians who inhabit a remote island far away in the midst of the sea ; the hundreds of thousands, (Commercial duties,) derived from the trade with their country concern not the Celestial Empire even to the extent of a hair of feather's down ; the possession is utterly unworthy of one careful thought. Their broad cloths and camelots are still more unimportant and of no regard.—But the tea, the rhubarb and the raw silk of the Inner Land are the sources by which they exist and support life. At the public Examination in the following month the acting Prefect was hooted by the students and driven out of the Examination Hall as a traitor.

Writhing under the smarting effects of the punishment they had brought upon themselves, the Officials were impatiently waiting for the departure of the forces that they might begin to rebuild the forts at the Bogue. They cared little for the warning they had received and had even commenced to renew some of the batteries, when H. M. S. Royalist, appearing on the scene one bright morning, immediately set to work and destroyed them again.

All this time the fleet had been busy in other directions as though to impress upon the Officials at the Coast-ports to the North the importance of the lessons administered at Canton. Amoy together with the island of Koolangsu, Chusan and Tinghai were captured. Chinhai and Ningpo were next occupied and many other exciting experiences too numerous to record in this brief sketch, were taking place.

The Chinese at last began to feel that the question of their supremacy over the rest of the world was in a fair way of being successfully disputed ; they therefore determined to prepare for a final struggle to settle the point for ever. To carry this decision into effect, many dastardly deeds were perpetrated by them : the crew and passengers of the transport "Nerbudda" which had gone ashore, were murdered. Captain Stead and the Captain of the British Barque " Anne " were also murdered. One of the Manchu officers was responsible for these outrages and on the matter being reported to the Emperor, this officer was promoted and the horrible deeds gloated over throughout the Empire.

On their now realizing the fact that the barbarians had captured Tinghai, Chinhai and Ningpo, the more northern Chinese began to doubt the utility of pressing their assertion of boasted supremacy any further, but the Cantonese still persevered in their efforts of preparation for a renewal of the war. The passage of the river was now obstructed by the sinking of junks laden with stones. The gunpowder factories and cannon foundries were kept very busy. Many new forts had been constructed under the advice of *certain foreigners* and 30,000 men were being constantly drilled in musketry.

Sir Henry Pottinger, regardless of this great display of energy on the part of the Chinese, was very firm in his policy. He again warned the officials at Canton that any attempt to reconstruct the forts at the Bogue would bring down on that city a severe punishment. The time for the completion of all these preparations pointed to the month of March, when hostilities were once more to begin.

An effort was also being made, and not without some success, to disaffect the rapidly increasing native population of Hongkong. Some 3,000 were said to have given their promise to rise upon a certain signal against the British, a leader for this scheme having been chosen by the Emperor, with the sudden massacre of all foreigners as the programme.

About this time Nankin was being seriously threatened by some the British ships, and as a consequence, the notable who had been chosen as leader for the Hongkong conspiracy, was suddenly recalled, so that the contemplated rising did not come off.

In the following February the Cantonese Officials ventured negotiations with some of the representatives of the *foreign element* for the construction of war-ships wherewith to operate against the British; but suspicions arose completely demoralizing this good intention, and the foreign representatives, being considered as little better than spies, the negotiations came to nothing.

By this time the fleet were all well up the Yangtsze, and after the fall of Woosung and Shanghai a speedy termination of the war seemed imminent.

Terms of peace were now offered by the Chinese Commissioners but these further peace negotiations were delayed, pending the assurance that the parties were properly authorized to act.

Finally, all their grievances were set forth by the British with demands for losses and compensation, terms of International Equality, and a cession of insula territory for Commerce and as a security for future good faith and behaviour.

The steady advance of the combined forces had gradually reduced the Chinese mind to a state of terror, and public opinion,—although it was plainly visible that the war was against the Government, the people not being molested in any way,—now began to turn in favour of peace with England.

To forward the interests of this happy issue, the Emperor was surreptitiously informed that the Cantonese were all in league with the foreigners, and, when in the ordinary course of astronomical occurrences, an eclipse of the sun transpired, the Officials were one and all in a dreadful state of despair, believing that even the great Orb of Light was against them.

The British fleet was now rapidly approaching Nankin and, as if in direful anticipation, three Commissioners came out from that city to negociate for terms of peace, but were told first to procure the Emperor's sanction to the British demands. This admitted of further Celestial procrastination and it was not until troops had actually landed for the assault that an armistice was arranged and then only to allow time for the Emperor's sanction to be obtained. A special messenger was despatched to Peking and on his return, all being in order, the Treaty of Nankin was, on August 29th 1842, duly concluded.

By the terms of this Treaty, the ports of Canton, Amoy, Foochow, Ningpo and Shanghai were thrown open to Foreign Trade, the cession of Hongkong was confirmed, payment of many further charges for loss to merchants was provided for, another indemnity of $6,000,000 with $12,000,000 more for war expenses was settled, as well as sundry other details of a minor character.

Hongkong was to be an absolutely free port, as will be seen by the following declaration.

" *It being obviously necessary and desirable that British subjects should have some port whereat they may careen and refit theirs ships when required and keep stores for that purpose. His Majesty the Emperor of China cedes to Her Majesty the Queen of Great Britain, &c., the Island of Hongkong to be possessed in perpetuity by Her Britannic Majesty, her heirs and successors, and to be governed by such laws and regulations as Her Majesty the Queen of Great Britain, &c., shall see fit to direct.*"

Finally, after one more quibble over the supremacy question, in which the Emperor was informed that the Queen of England acknowledged no superior or governor but God ; the Chinese Viceroy Ki-king admitted in his correspondence that "the Two Countries were united in the bonds of friendship."

The conclusion of the Nankin treaty at once dispelled the necessity for further warlike preparations, and as the campaign was considered to be at an end, the British forces both Military and Naval returned home.

China *at last* was obliged to bid her magnates come down from their assumed eminences. Her wall of isolation and conceit was shattered beyond the possibility of restoration. Her rulers apparently submitted with a good grace to all these humiliating experiences, which had proved to be the only effectual means of compelling them to abandon their ridiculous pretentions.

This was the fourth lesson she had received within three years ; this time it was certainly a very thorough one, and nothing further occurred to disturb the peaceful development of the new little Colony under the several administrations of Sir H. Pottinger who retired in 1844, Sir J. F. Davis from May 8th, 1844, to March 18th, 1848, Sir S. G. Bonham from March 20th, 1848 to April 2nd 1854, beyond the usual petty trivialities between the ever varying divisions and subdivisions *ad. inf.* of English Society.

The next governor was Sir John Bowring whose administration, commencing in April, 1854, at once promised to be an interesting epoch in the history of this now important British Outpost. The population by this time (13 years) had increased to over 50,000, and, owing to the disturbed state of the neighbouring mainland was still going ahead.

The first noticeable event, a Commercial Treaty with Siam, was very cleverly concluded by Sir John, from which dates the remarkable advance made by that nation in the western arts of Peace and Progress.

His diplomatic efforts with the Chinese were not so fortunate. When he made an attempt to approach the high Officials at the Capital he was cooly received by some of the deputies of the Viceroy of Chilhi, the high Officials still persisting in a haughty exclusivism.

The Taiping rebellion was raging about this time, and Sir John Bowring was for assisting in the suppression of the rebels, but there were so many sides to this obviously difficult question.

This serious trouble contributed much to augment the growth of the Colony, as the wealthier classes, especially from the neighbourhood of Canton, were all flocking to Hongkong for safety.

Viceroy Yeh remained supreme in his official position at that city, and, a newly appointed Consul arriving, Sir John addressed a despatch to His Excellency by way of introduction, which despatch was allowed to remain unnoticed for a month, when Sir John was curtly informed by the Viceroy that there was no precedent for acknowledging any despatch of that nature.

Celestial exclusivism still to the fore.

A storm was brooding again and one more lesson would have to be given to these Cantonese Officials in spite of what had already been done. A day of reckoning had to come for adjusting all matters of Treaty rights, and for demanding reparation for insults that were continually being heaped upon the European residents. At Canton the Treaty of Nankin was openly disregarded, owing it is supposed, to the close proximity of that city to Hongkong.

Viceroy Yeh was a very defiant character, and proved just the sort of man to bring matters to a speedy crisis. Owing to his dogged and determined disposition he was idolized by the gentry and literati of the province, who had erected in his honour a granite tablet inscribed with the following. *" Whilst all the people yielded to the barbarians, only we in Canton have ever destroyed them, cut them in pieces ; even our tender children long to devour their flesh and to sleep on their skins."*

This is Chinese poetry, and Yeh no doubt greatly appreciated such ennobling sentiments. One thing certain, His Excellency dreaded the power, and detested the commerce and the civilization of the West, even more than any of his predecessors had done. Although not aggressive, he steadfastly persisted in maintaining the supremacy of China over all barbarians ; he would have no interviews of any sort,—he would simply dictate his terms.

Yet, let us not laugh at this vain assumption when we remember China's ages of isolation from the rest of the world, and the fact that for many centuries previous to our own renaissence, she was perhaps the most civilized nation on earth. She knew the compass and the printing press when we were little better than savages, and even. at the present day we might learn not a little from her social organization. Her's is a civilization which she may well be excused for feeling proud and jealous of, it having been handed down through so many centuries and having outlived so many other and great civilizations.

The anti-foreign feeling in Canton increased during Yeh's term of office, although to some extent whilst the rebel troops were in the district, it remained hidden. But directly the city was considered secure from the possibilities of disturbance, the Canton gentry again showed themselves: insults were liberally heaped upon Europeans, Englishmen were hooted and stoned, and in fact it became plainly visible that a fifth lesson would have to be administered,—the impending crisis had at last arrived.

About this time the British flag was once more insulted by the forcible arrest of the crew of the British ship "Arrow" which occurrence formed a fitting opportunity for adjusting all longstanding grievances, and for bringing Mister Yeh to his bearings.

Sir John Bowring commenced by at once demanding a public surrender of the crew of the "Arrow" with an apology, which demands were both refused. On receipt of this curt refusal, 24 hours' notice was given to allow of the ship's crew being put on board, when twelve of the crew, instead of being put on board, were sent to the Consulate, but apology was still withheld. Admiral Seymour was now invited to take a hand in the game and commenced by demanding of Yeh a formal apology. Yeh insolently refused this demand and the Admiral forthwith destroyed two of the forts, and then gave another chance to the obstinate Viceroy, but of no avail. The Official residence was then destroyed, which was also of no avail. The next day the city wall was breeched right opposite to the Official residence, but Yeh had retired to another quarter inside, and had defied the Admiral to do his worst.

Following this, the Civil Governor's as also the Tartar General's residences were destroyed, Admiral Seymour supposing that these officials would prevail on Yeh to act sensibly, but it was no good, he still held out.

After this, other of the forts including the Bogue once more, were reduced but without any result whatever.

Not having sufficient force—the Admiral now retired to Hongkong and informed Sir John of what had happened as also of the position, and then applied home for 5,000 men.

Both the Chinese and European residents at Hongkong were much dismayed at these proceedings.

It was now Yeh's innings—he offered Tls. 100 for English heads, and called upon the Chinese at Hongkong to leave the colony, but first to avenge his wrongs by dagger, poison and fire, or by any means in their power, however diabolical.

In Hongkong this appeal had no effect, the Chinese, now so long accustomed to British rule, knew when they were well off, but in Canton all the establishments were destroyed, and at Whampoa the docks and store-houses were burned.

Yeh's machinations were not altogether without some effect, as the residents of Hongkong were held in a constant state of terror, crimes against Europeans and their property being of hourly occurrence,—there was a daily chronicle of "Chinese atrocities."

On January 15th, 1857, the bread was poisoned, but fortunately, there being too great a quantity of the deleterious matter, *Arsenic*, used, the effect was only that of a very unpleasant emetic and no immediate deaths were caused by the poisoning.

On this never-to-be-forgotten morning the excitement in the Colony was intense. Martial law was now demanded and every chinaman who could not answer for his respectability was to be deported,—*but*, after all nothing was done.

On the news of all the foregoing troubles reaching home, Viceroy Yeh was at first looked upon as a martyr, a very much illused man ; however, his record of humane acts, which had also appeared in the home papers, finally appealed to the sympathies of the English people, and preparations were forthwith ordered to be made for another expedition,—*another lesson.*

In the meantime the crew of another British ship had been murdered; fires of a very suspicious character were of common occurrence in the Colony and the natives were again ordered to quit the place, but with little result.

British shipping was also being continually harassed, and even British gunboats, until Yeh's naval head-quarters and a fleet of war-junks were destroyed in Fatshan Creek, had occasionally suffered.

In July 1857, the Lord Elgin expedition arrived bringing with it a recognizable modicum of reserved prejudice, as his Lordship appeared to have considerable sympathy with the position of Viceroy Yeh.

Lord Elgin was a grand specimen of the true British nobleman, a humane man with a nature illadapted for his profession. In his correspondence, he has expressed himself as feeling sad indeed to think that he should have to execute orders which would, in their effect, cause so much distress and desolation, where all around perfect peace and tranquility appeared to reign supreme: however, to arrest that terrible malignant growth of Celestial selfishness, measures of the severest possible nature seemed to be unavoidable.

The programme was to be a full one. Compensation for infringement of Treaty rights, and the establishing of a Legation at Peking, were the two principal items.

After a somewhat tedious delay, pending the conclusion of negociations which never came off, it was deemed advisable to resort to pressure, so the Canton River was once more blockaded by the British fleet.

Fully a year had elapsed since Admiral Seymour retired from Canton for want of a sufficient force, and during this interval of suspense, the stubborn Viceroy had busied himself, according to his own ideas, with strengthening his position.

At last a despatch formulating the British demands was sent to him, to which, after a delay of ten days, a reply was received that at once confirmed the character of the man. He promised nothing,—but was willing that everything should go on as heretofore.

He was determined to avoid the slightest show of submission or even of common courtesy to the barbarian invaders.

By this time some 5,000 British troops and 900 French mostly marines, were in the neighbourhood of Canton, and on December 24th, 1857, an ultimatum was forwarded giving 24 hours for compliance with the British demands. Yeh again assumed a menacing attitude of obstinacy, and his reply to the ultimatum was altogether evasive, so without any further waste of time, the bombardment of the City was once more commenced on the 28th of that month.

The artillery fire was confined to the walls and forts and to the quarter in which the Official Yamens were situated.

While all this destruction was going on, Yeh, as if to obtain some satisfaction out of the performance, was rehearsing a little drama on his own account,—executing Chinese rebels; (his score is stated to have been many thousand heads); he remained quite insensible to the effects of the British operations. With very little resistance the troops in due course entered the city and a party of British bluejackets bursting into the official Yamen collared the old Viceroy as a prisoner whilst he was in the act of making his escape over a wall at the back.

This wonderful tyrant, Viceroy Yeh, could boast that he had never interviewed a European, that he had never even met one face to face before, and alas, what an ignominious position in which to find himself.

Canton was now completely in the hands of the troops, and the question soon arose as to what to do with the City and its Viceroy. It was seen that nothing could be begun satisfactorily with Yeh's presence amongst them, so he was forthwith deported to Calcutta where after the lapse of two years, during which he had ample time to repent of his long list of misdeeds, he departed this life. The city of Canton was held by the allied forces and governed by a mixed Commission for nearly four years afterwards.

Thus ended the fifth lesson, their southern Capital and their Viceroy captured,—a very sorry one indeed for the Celestials again to receive at the hands of those dreadful barbarians.

Let us hope, that in future, *our* lessons to this vast Empire will be *all* confined to the Arts of peace.

Affairs in Hongkong remained in a very unsettled state until the departure of Sir John Bowring, continued efforts being regularly made by the Canton Officials to excite the Chinese inhabitants against the Europeans. The people in the country were urged by the Mandarins, under severe threats, to command their freinds, residents in Hongkong, at once to leave the place; and many there were who resigned lucrative situations to obey these commands, knowing that untold vengance would otherwise be wreaked upon their families in the interior. Market supplies were again interfered with and the Europeans once more felt they were being boycotted. During all this period of outside disturbances; the Colony, now fast approaching the age of manhood, was in the throes of great internal disorder amongst the Officials, who were squabling between themselves and with one another, over all sorts of petty grievances, to the damage of the public service and to the injury of the Colony's reputation in the eyes of the outside world. This disgraceful state of affairs was characterized in the London Times of the period as "a storm in a teapot."

Sir John Bowring during his term of administration, succeeded in doubling the revenue of the Colony, although at the same time the expenditure was very large. Piracy on the high sea, as might have been expected, during such exciting times, was rampant, in spite of the efforts of the British men-of-war, which, as time and opportunity permitted, were not altogether inactive as the following extraordinary record will show. About 100 junks, 1,400 men, 20 snake-boats, 1 battery, 134 large guns besides a whole fleet of war-junks were destroyed.

Thirty-two piratical attacks were recorded within 15 weeks.

At this period of history, so vigorous and effective had been the policy of Sir John, fostering the growth of security to life and property, that the population of the Colony increased some 20,000 in two about years, making an extraordinary total of over 75,000 souls from the date of occupation, eighteen years previous. The Commerce of the Colony, especially with Siam, flourished throughout this administration. Japan and the Philippines also came well to the front, and Chinese emigration to California and Australia, the principal markets for labour, went rapidly ahead. The Colony had attained to the position of the leading Commercial Emporium of the East, and at the same time ranked in importance as the first seaport in the Pacific. The shipping returns had risen during the five years from 300,000 to 700,000 tons, square rigged merchantmen, and the native junk trade increased in like proportion.

Sir John Bowring left the Colony much respected by the Chinese although blamed by the European Press. On his arrival in England he received the well merited thanks of the Ministry for his faithful and patient services in Hongkong.

In his memoirs he has written.—"I have been severely blamed for the policy I pursued in China, yet that policy has proved most beneficial to my country and to mankind in general. It is not fair or just to suppose that a course of action which might be practicable or prudent at home can always succeed abroad."

The great work accomplished by Sir John Bowring tells its own story at the present day.

Sir Hercules Robinson next succeeded as Governor of the Colony from September 9th, 1859 to March 15th, 1865 and considering the period of extraordinary advance and development which it was his good fortune to have to follow on, it is not at all surprising to find a continuance of the same measure of good times which had been so ably inaugurated by his predecessor Sir John Bowring. Sir Hercules was undoubtedly an able governor both as a financier as well as an allround hardworker, and under such auspices a heathly public spirit naturally prevailed. Amongst other achievements, a substantial praya wall, a clock-tower, the drinking fountain opposite to the City Hall and the City Hall itself with public library, theatre and assembly rooms, as also the public gardens and many more like undertakings were completed during this administration.

Crime on shore and piracy on the high seas, owing it might be supposed to the carelessness consequent on the exceptional prosperity, was also demanding the fullest attention of the Authorities. The population at this period, 1865, was 125,000.

During the next seventeen years under the several administrations of Sir R. G. MacDonald, March 15th, 1865 to April 22nd, 1872, Sir Arthur Kennedy April 16th, 1872 to March 1st, 1877, Sir John Pope Hennessy, April 22nd, 1877 to March 7th, 1882 with several short intervals of interregnum there is little to record beyond the ordinary peaceful growth of commerce, population, both European and native, and public works both useful and ornamental. These speak for themselves.

1881.—Population ............; 160,000
        Shipping ...............2,853,279 tons.
        Junk trade ...........1,680,025 tons.

The next governor appointed was Sir George Ferguson Bowen from March 30th, 1883 to December 19th, 1885 during whose period of administration the condition of the Colony from the aspect of hygiene, received considerable and careful attention, especially in matters of house building and drainage, food supply, and general cleanliness. A Sanitary Board was established possessing extensive authority. The great water supply of the colony Tytam reservoir, dam, tunnel and conduit were rapidly pushed ahead, and have, owing to the continued enormous increase of the population, proved an incalculable boon.

About this period war broke out between France and China considerably affecting the port of Hongkong, and at one time causing a temporary stoppage of the supplies of fruit and vegetables, owing to the boat-people and coolies, licensed carriers, refusing to work for the French Mail-service, thereby abusing the rights and conditions of their licenses. This trouble is supposed to have been caused by the influence of the Canton Officials.

The question of the blockade of the colony by the Revenue Cruisers of the Chinese Imperial Maritime Custom's Service was very carefully discussed and finally adjusted, *to the immediate prejudice of the freedom of the port*, so far as the junk trade was concerned : however, after the new system had been some time in operation and had become properly understood; the junk people began to recognize certain benefits in the shape of security to their trade and to their property. The new system helped to establish the observance of maritime trading rules, by giving to each vessel its proper status, which hitherto had not been done.

The ultimate effect was to protect the honest trader by making the operations of the pirate as the smuggler much more difficult.

The next governor was Sir William Des Vœux from October 6th, 1887 to 7th May, 1891, during whose period of administration on the 9th November, 1887, the Queen's Jubilee was celebrated in magnificient style. There was much feasting and rejoicing and a fund for the erection of a Jubilee Memorial Statue of Her Majesty, was inaugurated.

The Chinese are said to have collected and spent $100,000 in the festivities of this celebration.

The Praya Reclamation, whereby an addition to the building land of the colony right along the foreshore of the harbour, measuring in extent about 57 acres including a praya 70 feet wide, was begun ; the Memorial Stone being laid by H. R. H. Duke of Connaught on the 2nd April, 1890.

On the 21st to 23th January, 1891 the celebration of the Hongkong Jubilee took place amidst great rejoicing. Fifty years of Progress, Population 200,000, Merchant shipping *1890*, 13,334,820 tons,
(1840.—nil.)

The festivities were kept up for three days as public holidays, during which there was great feasting.

A Royal Salute was fired, a public ball given and a Naval and Military Review with atheletic sports and various other contests for all comers.

Governor Des Vœux left the colony 7th May, 1891, after a somewhat trying time owing to ill health, when, in due course the present Governor Sir William Robinson, K.C.M.G., came amongst us in the December of that year, and since his advent, with one exception, there has been little to mar the peace and prosperity of the colony, as the following figures from the Harbour Master's annual reports will testify.

From the Harbour Master's annual reports :—

| Year | British | Tons | Foreign | Tons | Junks | Tons | Total Tons |
|------|---------|------|---------|------|-------|------|------------|
| 1888 | 5,121 | 6,474,343 | 2,460 | 2,532,334 | 47,567 | 3,703,707 | 12,710,384 |
| 1889 | 5,212 | 6,500,869 | 2,376 | 2,471,121 | 45,568 | 3,417,331 | 12,389,321 |
| 1890 | 5,524 | 6,994,919 | 2,695 | 2,776,822 | 46,668 | 3,572,079 | 13,334,820 |
| 1891 | 5,719 | 7,190,589 | 2,988 | 3,088,454 | 45,403 | 3,263,118 | 13,842,161 |
| 1892 | 6,376 | 7,576,323 | 2,598 | 2,717,829 | 45,190 | 3,192,076 | 13,486,228 |
| 1893 | 6,128 | 7,732,195 | 2,630 | 2,803,664 | 47,197 | 3,488,007 | 14,023,866 |
| 1894 | 6,022 | 7,778,396 | 2,430 | 2,690,786 | 45,861 | 3,482,124 | 13,951,306 |
| 1895 | 6,626 | 8,589,637 | 2,463 | 2,935,949 | 53,027 | 3,683,700 | 15,209,286 |
| 1896 | 6,454 | 8,758,294 | 2,898 | 3,575,102 | 59,576 | 3,767,403 | 16,100,799 |

It is an interesting fact that the total tonnage entering and clearing at Hongkong in the year 1895, exceeded that of 1894 London—by 775,706 tons, also of 1894 Liverpool by 1,036,008 tons, and Cardiff by 1,047,195 tons; this is exclusive of local junk and home coasting trade.

In the Summer of last year there were two very serious typhoons one after the other doing great damage to the trees in the public gardens, and even snapping off the flagstaff at the peak which had never been known to occur before. The greatest force of the wind was gauged as 120 miles.—180 feet per second.

## STEAMSHIP SERVICES.

*See Advertisements at the beginning of Book.*

# CONSULATES AND CONSULS, 1897.

### AUSTRIA-HUNGARY.
Actg. Consul—G. HARLING.................... ........Praya Central.

### BELGIUM.
Consul—LEON VINCART .........................Robinson Road.

### BRAZIL.
Consul—A. G. ROMANO .......:........ ...........49, Wyndham Street.

### CHILE.
Consul—R. SHEWAN .............................Praya Central.

### DENMARK.
Actg. Consul—C. BEURMANN......................Praya Central.

### FRANCE.
Consul—LEON GME. LE ROUX ...............⎰
Vice-Consul—A. GIRAUD ......................⎱ Praya Central.

### HAWAII.
Actg. Conl.-General—Hon. J. J. BELL IRVING...Pedder Street.

### GERMANY.
Consul—L. VON LOEPER .......................8, Wyndham Street.

## ITALY.

Vice-Consul—V. P. Musso ...................Praya West.

## JAPAN.

Consul—S. Shimizu ........................29, Caine Road.

## NETHERLANDS.

Consul-General—F. J. Haver Droeze......}
Consul—J. J. Bysterus Heemskerk ......} 3, Wyndham Street.

## MEXICO.

Vice-Consul—Aug. J. do Rozario ............Stanley Street.

## PERU.

Consul-General—Don Felipe S. Meza.........9, Queen's Road.

## PORTUGAL.

Consul-General—A. G. Romano................49, Wyndham Street.

## RUSSIA.

Consul—St. C. Michaelsen ...................Praya Central.

## SIAM.

Consul—Hon. C. P. Chater ...................5 Queen's Road Central

## SPAIN.

Consul—Sr. Don Jose de Navaro ...........}
Vice-Consul—Don H. Gonzales del Castillo } 3, Arbuthnot Road.

## SWEDEN AND NORWAY.

Actg. Vice-Consul—G. Harling ...............3, Queen's Road.

## U. S. AMERICA.

Consul—Wm. E. Hunt .......................} "Burnbrae"
Vice-Consul—J. A. Hunt ....................}    Glencaly Road.

## MONEY.

Hongkong Silver dollars.

Mexican      „      „

Japanese      „    (yen.)

**Notes,** representing silver, of the first four of the Local Banks below.

**Gold** of any description can always be changed at the Banks, or at the native money-changers.

---

## BANKS.

The Hongkong and Shanghai Banking Corporation.

The Chartered Bank of India Australia and China.

The Mercantile Bank of India.

The National Bank of China.

The Bank of China and Japan.

The Agra Bank.

The Yokohama Specie Bank.

*(The Offices are all close to each other.)*

---

## POSTAL SERVICE.

The **General Post Office** situated next to the Clock Tower, where notices are posted every morning giving full particulars of the daily mail service, which particulars are also published in the daily papers.

Letter rates per ½ oz.

Canton and Macao, 2 cents ; Coast ports and Philippines, 5 cents ; Straits Settlements, Europe, Australia, Japan and the United States, 10 cents.

# VOCABULARY
## (IN THE LOCAL DIALECT).

NOTE.—You are advised to show the characters in preference to any attempt to pronounce them, as the right tones are difficult to give and a very slight error in *tone* may alter the meaning of the word.

| | | |
|---|---|---|
| Yes ! | 係 | Hai. |
| No ! | 冇 | Mò. |
| Cash | 錢 | Ts'in. |
| Dollars | 銀 | Ngan. |
| No. 1 | 壹 | Yat. |
| 2 | 弍 | I. |
| 3 | 叁 | Sám. |
| 4 | 肆 | Sz. |
| 5 | 伍 | Ng. |
| 6 | 陸 | Luk. |
| 7 | 柒 | Ts'at. |
| 8 | 捌 | Pát. |
| 9 | 玖 | Kau. |
| 10 | 拾 | Shap. |
| 11 | 十一 | Shap-yat. |
| 12 | 十二 | Shap-i. |
| 20 | 二十 | I-shap. |
| 30 | 三十 | Sám-shap. |
| 40 | 四十 | Sz-shap. |
| 50 | 五十 | Ng-shap. |
| 100 | 一佰 | Yat-pák. |

| | | |
|---|---|---|
| 1,000 .................. | 一千 | Yat-ts'in. |
| 10,000 .................. | 一萬 | Yat-mán. |
| Immediately ............ | 卽刻 | Tsik hák. |
| By and by .............. | 遲吓 | Chi 'há. |
| Many thanks ............ | 多謝吓 | To tsé. |
| Wait a little ............ | 等吓 | Tang há. |
| I want something to eat | 我要食野 | Ngo iü shik yé. |
| Please bring me | 多煩拈俾我 | To fán nim pi ngo. |
| Rice ..................... | 飯 | Fán. |
| Bread .................. | 麵飽 | Min páu. |
| Meat (beef) ............ | 凍牛肉 | Ngau yuk. |
| Fowl .................. | 鷄項 | Kai hong. |
| Fish ........ | 生魚 | Shang ü. |
| Eggs .................. | 鷄旦 | Kai-táu. |
| Biscuits .......... | 餅干 | Peng kon. |
| Oranges .......... | 柑橙 | Kom ch'áng. |
| Bananas .............. | 香芽蕉 | Héung ngá tsiú. |
| Tea .................. | 茶 | Ch'á. |
| Sugar .................. | 白糖 | Pák t'ong. |
| Wine .................. | 酒 | 'Tsau. |
| Salt .................. | 生鹽 | Sháng ím. |
| Knife (one) ............ | 一張刀仔 | Yat chéung tò tsai. |
| Fork    ,, ............ | 一枝义 | Yat chi ch'á. |
| Spoon .................. | 匙羹 | Shi kang. |
| Water .................. | 水 | Shui. |
| Hot Water ............ | 熱水 | Yit shui. |
| Cold Water ............ | 凍水 | Tung shui. |
| It is unnecessary ....... | 唔使 | M' shái. |

| | | |
|---|---|---|
| Be careful .............. | 小心 | Siú sam. |
| That will do ......... | 呢個做得 | Ni ko tsó tak. |
| Good morning ........ .. | 早晨 | Tsó shan. |
| I want to buy (some-thing.) ...... ...... | 我要買的野 | Ngo iú mái tik yét. |
| Porcelain ............... | 瓦器 | Ngá hi. |
| Old embroideries ....... | 舊顧繡 | Kau kú sau. |
| New embroideries ...... | 新顧繡 | San kú sau. |
| Ivory-ware ............. | 象牙器 | Tséung nga hi. |
| Bronzes .............. | 古玩 | Kú ún. |
| Blackwood furniture ... | 酸枝檯椅 | Sün chí t'oi í. |
| Silk ................. | 綢緞 | Ch'au tün. |
| Handkerchief ........... | 手巾 | Shau kan. |
| Shawls ................. | 搭膊巾 | Táp pok kan. |
| Curios ............... | 古玩 | Kú mún. |
| Jade-stone ............. | 玉器 | Yuk hi. |
| What is the price? ...... | 幾多價錢 | Ki to ká ts'in. |
| Too dear ............... | 太貴 | T'ái kwai. |
| Will you take less? ...... | 減少的 | Kám siú tik. |
| I am satisfied ........... | 就咁略 | Tsau kòm lok. |
| Be quick .............. | 快的 | Fái tik. |
| This is mine ............ | 係我嘅 | Hai ngo ké. |
| Put in paper ........... | 俾紙包好 | Pí chi páu hó. |
| Pack it up in wood case | 俾箱庄好 | Pí séung chong hó. |
| That will do ....... ..... | 做得 | Tsó tak. |
| I must go .............. | 我定要去 | Ngo teng iú hü. |
| I am .............. | 我係 | Ngo hai. |
| English ............... | 英國人 | Ying kwok yan. |

| | | |
|---|---|---|
| French | 法國人 | Fát kwok yan. |
| German | 德國人 | Tak kwok yan. |
| American | 花旗人 | Fá k'i yan. |
| Portuguese | 西洋人 | Sai yéung yan. |
| Take me to | 仝我去 | T'ung ngo hü. |
| French Consul | 法國領事 | Fát kwok ling sz. |
| German Consul | 德國領事 | Tak kwok ling sz. |
| American Consul | 花旗領事 | Fá k'i ling sz. |
| Portugese Consul | 西洋領事 | Sai yéung ling sz. |
| Hongkong Hotel | 香港酒店 | Héung kong tsau tím. |
| Mount Austin Hotel | 山頂大酒店 | Shan tang tai tsau tím. |
| Queen's Road | 皇后大道 | Wong hau-tai-to. |
| Public Gardens | 兵頭花園 | Ping tau fa uen. |
| Happy Valley | 黄坭涌 | Wong nai tsung. |
| Pok-fo-lum | 博葫林 | Pok fo lum. |
| Ty tam | 大潭 | Tai-tam. |
| Stanley | 赤柱 | Chek chu. |
| City Hall | 薛地苛 | Sit-ti-ho. |
| Ceneral Police Station | 大館 | Tai kwún. |
| Central Market | 中環街市 | Tsung wan kai shi. |
| Canton Steamer | 省城火船 | Shang sheng fo shün. |
| Go with me | 仝我去 | T'ung ngo hü. |
| Do not trouble me | 勿運我 | Mat wan ngo. |
| I do not require you | 我唔使你 | Ngo m shai ni. |
| Do not hurt me | 勿打我 | Mat tá ngo. |
| Be patient | 忍耐 | Yan noi. |
| I beg pardon | 唔該 | M koi. |
| He did it on purpose | 佢特意做 | K'ü tak i tsò. |

| English | Chinese | Romanization |
|---|---|---|
| What is that to you? ... | 於你何干 | U ni ho kon. |
| Good-bye ............. | 好行拉 | Hò hang lái. |
| Come and see me ....... | 來見我 | Loi kin ngo. |
| What time is it? ...... | 幾點鐘 | Kí tím chung. |
| Five o'clock ........... | 五點鐘 | Ng tim chung. |
| Half past six .......... | 六點半 | Luk tim pún. |
| What place is this?...... | 係乜野地方 | Hai mat yét tí fong. |
| Show me where they are ................ | 話我知係邊處 | Wá ngo chí hai pin chü. |
| Carry this ............. | 拈呢的野 | Nim ni tik yé. |
| Be very careful ........ | 小心的 | Siú sam tik. |
| Come again at........... | 再來過 | Tsoi loi kwo. |
| To-morrow morning ... | 明朝早 | Ming ch'iú tsó. |
| I will reward you ..... | 賞你 | (Ngo) shéung ni. |
| Hurry away............. | 行快的 | Hang fái tik. |

# PLACES OF INTEREST.

The Clock Tower, a square granite structure about 80 feet high, situated in the centre of the City of Victoria at the Queen's Road end of Pedder's Street, between the Hongkong Hotel and the General Post Office, was erected by public subscription about the year 1860.

It supports a well regulated clock and a fire-bell, and may be considered as the best land-mark in the Colony.

The General Post Office will be found on the corner of Queen's Road and Pedder's Street. Particulars of Steamer arrivals are exhibited by a system of movable boards on the Queen's Road front.

Purchasers of Postage Stamps should apply at least an hour before the advertized time for the closing of the mail for which they intend their letters, as the crush of native servants on the approach of mail-closing hour is, in many cases, very objectionable, and not unfrequently dangerous.

The Supreme Court House, formerly the Old Exchange Building, situated next to the General Post Office, was purchased from a merchant firm in 1847. During the Sessions which commence their sittings on the 18th of every month, a peep into these, generally to be avoided precincts, may interest the sightseer.

The City Hall situated off Queen's Road a little further to the eastward close to the Cricket and Parade Grounds, was erected by public subscription about the year 1865. The most interesting of its many features in the museum, where a varied collection of local and tropical specimens of birds, reptiles and insects, as also minerals, together with many other curiosities of native handiwork, will admit of a pleasant hour being spent.

A valuable library and reading room are to be found adjoining the museum, where, for those who may be curious, a complete record, in the Government Official Gazette dating from 1841, of the Colony's progress in every department, will be found.

There is also a very pretty theatre, and several spacious assembly rooms suitable for receptions, public meetings, balls, &c.

The Chamber of Commerce holds its sittings within this building.

The **Hongkong and Shanghai Bank** is situated next to the City Hall in a substantial granite structure of magnificent proportions and of fine architectural design (classical). This is one of the many institutions which speaks wonders for the remarkable progress of the Colony.

**Government House** is situated on one of the spurs from the northern slope of Mount Victoria just below the Public Gardens, and commands extensive views in every direction. It is at present the Official Residence of Governor Sir William Robinson, K.C.M.G. and Mountain View at the peak is the Summer Residence.

**Head-Quarter House** situated to the eastward of Government House, also at the extremity of a smaller spur from Mount Gough, is the Official Residence of the Military Officer in command for the time being. Standing in its own grounds in close proximity with the barracks, this residence forms a prominent feature viewed from the man-of-war anchorage.

**St. John's Protestant Cathedral** situated immediately above the Military Parade-ground was erected about

1847 having the addition of a new chancel in 1869, the foundation stone of which was laid by H.R.H. the Duke of Edinburgh. The interior is like that of most Cathedrals with very pretty effect produced by the stained glass windows to be seen in every direction. It is capable of seating about 800 people.

The Government Offices are situated close to St. John's Cathedral, and include the Council Chamber as well as the accommodation for departmental staff. The Director of public works, the Surveyor General, occupies the ground floor of the building.

The Roman Catholic Cathedral (Church of the Immaculate Conception) is situated up the hill at the top of Glenealy Ravine, and to the right of the public Gardens. It is a modern *cruciform* structure of considerable dimensions and from its elevated position is very plainly seen from the harbour.

The Union Church, at present situated on Kennedy Road, has a history of its own. Originally erected in 1845, in the centre of the City in Hollywood Road, it was in 1863 trasferred to Elgin Street, where, suffering from that fatal disease which attacks so many tropical Protestant Institutions in the Far East, it all but expired. Revival again set in and the building in Elgin Street, with considerable improvements as regards ventilation, was transferred to the present site. It is capable of seating about 500 people.

Queen's College formerly the Government Central School is situated in the centre of a district thickly populated by Chinese. It is a very spacious building capable of accommodating 1,000 scholars. The fees are from $1 to $3 per month.

The Italian Convent situated on Caine Road is perhaps the most to be admired of all the practically useful institutions in the Colony.  Founded at Verona by the Marchioness Canossa in the year 1808, (and in Hongkong, in 1860) as "The Daughters of Charity Canossean" and having for its object, the protection and education of the children (*girls*) of the people, regardless of creed or colour: during the past 37 years it has been the means of alleviating much distress and suffering amongst the families of the poorer classes, besides its educational efforts to implant the seeds of kindness and orderly living in the minds and dispositions of the young.  Its departments are many.  There are day schools, boarding schools, native orphan schools, a foundling ward, a Catechumenate, a home for the aged poor women; and, a special establishment for Magdalens including a hospital for the sick ; in all six separate houses in the Colony.  The standard of its teaching is in every respect up to the requirements of the Government Education Department. so that, according to the success attained at the periodical examinations, it participates in the Grant-in-aid scheme.  As accomplishments—languages, music, drawing and the most beautiful of embroidery, lace and fancy needlework, are taught.  The number of its inmates is about 600 and it receives on an average over 1.000 foundlings every year.  Visiting the sick, and occasionally nursing are also amongst its voluntary duties.

Further, there are many branches in the East and Far East—3 in India, 2 in Timor, 1 in Singapore, 1 in Hankow, and 2 in Macao.

The entire establishment is managed solely by ladies of various nationality.  Italians, French, German Austrian, Spanish and Portuguese, who, as the Voluntary Daughters of Charity, devote their lives to the noble work of protecting and educating the children of the poor. Its means of subsistance are for the most part from private teaching, the sale of needlework, and from the school fees,—occasionally augmented by the contribution of some generous donor, and the kind and gratuitous assistance of the Medical profession.

La Maison de Nazareth, one of the establishments of the Société des Missions-Etrangères founded at Paris in the year 1660, occupies the much enlarged premises of the Old Douglas Castle at Pokfolum. The great and very important work undertaken by this Society is Evangelistic training and Religious instruction amongst the various nations of the Far East, and throughout every province of the Chinese Empire. In the execution of this work. the establishment operates a type foundry and an extensive printing office where books are published in most of the Asiatic languages, and sometimes in hitherto unknown tongues. The Mission even goes so far as to invent, design, and establish characters for written language where, as is occasionally discovered, no such alphabetical system has ever before existed.

This useful and *Model* institution at Pokfolum, is unique in every respect, and in doing the afternoon walk from the Peak (Programme No. 1) half-an-hour may be very pleasantly spent in seeing over the place. The many branches of the Mission-Etrangères and the object and extent of their labours are perhaps the widest of any of the Foreign Missions in this part of the world. The French Fathers have always a hearty welcome for everyone.

The Hongkong Club, situated on the New Prava, overlooking the harbour to the North, and the Cricket Ground to the South, is a magnificent edifice of five stories. It is designed in the later Italian style of Architecture, surmounted by three lightly constructed cupolas, which contribute to relieve the proportions of the mainbuilding, at the same time producing a very pretty and finished effect. Perfect in its arrangements, it provides every accommodation and ammusement that can possibly be conceived as necessary or desirable in such an institution.

The Memorial Statue of Her Majesty The Queen, situated about the centre of the New Reclamation close to the Hongkong Club, was erected in commemoration of the Jubilee year of Her Majesty's Reign (9th November 1887.) The unveiling of the monument took place on the 28th May, 1896 in the presence of a vast assemblage of residents representing many nationalities. His Excellency, Governor Sir William Robinson, assisted by the Members of Council, Representatives of Army and Navy and Heads of Departments, performed the ceremony, amidst the firing of a *fue de joie*, the playing of military bands, and a general show of rejoicing and acclamation from the people.

The Club Germania, situated in Wyndham Street is, in its provision for its members, the same as the Hongkong Club previously described. It was erected by and belongs to the German Section of the community as its name supplies.

The Hongkong Observatory, situated at Kowloon on the Southern slope of Mount Elgin is kept up for the purpose of Meteorological Observations and Record, so very necessary during the Typhoon Season from May until September inclusive. A time-ball above the little round tower at Chim-sa-choy, Kowloon Point, is operated from the Observatory by electricity every day at 1 p.m. Whether reports and forecasts are also issued daily by this institution.

St. Joseph's College is situated on Robinson Road above the Roman Catholic Cathedral and helps to make up that imposing pile of buildings so prominently seen from the harbour. The College is under the control of the Christian Brothers, is very ably conducted and provides mostly for the education of the Portuguese section of the community.

St. Paul's College, situated in Albert Road close to the Glenealy Ravine, dates back to the early days in the History of the Colony and is principally devoted to the education of the better class Chinese youth with a view to their becoming useful as interpreters in the Government Service.

It has long been under the control of the local Protestant Missionary Bishop, hence little is known as to its working or its progressive results.

The Diocesan Home and Orphanage, situated on Bonham Road was started in the year 1859, by Bishop Smith, as a native training school. It attains to about the same measure of success as the St. Paul's College, being under the same directorship.

The French Convent (Asile de la St. Enfance) situated on the Praya to the Eastward having also an entrance in Queen's Road East, was founded in Paris prior to the French Revolution (in Hongkong in 1848), as "Les Sœurs de Charité de St. Paul de Chartres." It comprises day and boarding schools and its educational attainments are up to the requirements of the Government Education Department. It has also a native Orphanage and provides for the aged poor. Its means of support are obtained by the sale of needlework as also from the school fees and the Government-grant. It has in the Far East—5 branch establishments in Japan, and 5 also in Tonquin. In Hongkong the number of its inmates is 350.

The Docks, of which there are three distinct establishments all belonging to the Hongkong and Whampoa Dock Co., Ld. are situated respectively at Hungham Kowloon Bay, known as the Kowloon Docks; at Samsuipo on the West of the Kowloon Peninsula known as the Cosmopolitan Docks; and also at Aberdeen on the southern side of the Island of Hongkong, known as the Aberdeen Docks.  To those interested in Shipbuilding and Engineering-work on an extensive scale, a visit to any of these establishments can be arranged through the courtesy of the Company's Manager and Secretary.

The Club Lusitano, situated in Shelley Street provides for the Portuguese Community just as the Hongkong Club and the Club Germania do for the British and German residents.  A good Concert room, library, reading rooms and billiard rooms form the principal features of the establishment.

The Baxter Protestant Mission School, "Fairlea" situated on Bonham Road takes its name from Miss Harriet Baxter who in 1860 came to Hongkong as honorary Missionary of the Society for promoting Female Education in the East.  Its work is first educational,—with a large Boarding School for Chinese and Eurasian children, also a day school having an attendance of nearly 200 scholars. In addition its efforts are Evangelistic.  It has its own little church and special school services with a number of Bible women visiting daily and having access to a considerable section of the native families in their homes.

The Basel Mission, situated in Western Street and having an entrance in High Street, was founded in 1847 with the object of educating and training the heathen in many lands for Evangelistic work.  It maintains a middle school for general subjects and a higher school for the study of theology. It also supports a girls school mustering some eighty scholars; the standard of teaching being up to the requirements of the Government Education Department.

Far away about 25 miles north, in the Sun On district this Mission also controls a hospital and a medical staff; and has established throughout the same district 12 Stations for preparing preachers and teachers for work amongst the Hakkas. Besides this the Mission has many branches in India, The Gold Coast, West Africa, and the Cameroons.

**The Berlin Foundling House,** situated in High Street, off Bonham Road, was founded by the Berlin Ladies Mission in the year 1861. The first lady missionary from this society arrived in Hongkong in 1850 and resided for a time at Morrison Hill, the centre of Educational and Mission Work at that period.

As its name implies, the Mission had in view the saving of those female children which, by long established custom, the native mothers have been brought up to discard, throw away, abandon, leave on the road side to die. In Chinese family life the female off-spring is thought little of, and should she be allowed to live, has, through her years of girlhood, without the slightest effort to educate her, to act as a general drudge for the rest of the family. This is more particularly when she is not considered sufficiently good-looking for the cultivation of small feet.

On a child entering the Foundling House it becomes the property, so to speak, of the Mission, who educate and train her to a useful life, and in a great many cases, see her comfortably settled as the wife of an educated native preacher of one of the many societies doing Mission work in the neighbourhood.

The institution is supported by the generosity of patrons at home and in the Colony.

The Reformatory School and Orphanage, situated at West Point, started by Father T Raimondi of the Italian Mission in 1864 and now under the control of the Vicar Apostolic,—provides education in the native tongue for Chinese boys from the age of eight years. It also takes in and cares for the deaf, the dumb and the blind, and in cases of reformatory treatment finds occupation for its inmates in the learning of useful trades.

The Government Civil Hospital, situated to the West, off the Queen's Road about a mile from the Clock Tower, was first organized in the year 1848. It includes, after many additions, very extensive premises, with separate departments for different ailments, also a handsome residence standing in its own grounds for the Medical Officer in charge and a very spacious building for the use of the European nursing staff.

The Alice Memorial Hospital, situated in Staunton Street, was founded about 1882 by Dr. Ho Kai to the memory of the late Mrs. Ho Kai. It is at present under the management of the London Missionary Society and provides chiefly for Chinese patients.

The Nethersole Hospital, situated on Caine Road, is similar in its provisions to the Alice Memorial Hospital being also under the control of the London Missionary Society.

The Happy Valley, situated to the Eastward about half an hour's walk from the Clock Tower, was much favoured as a place of public resort as far back as 1845; the first driving road to run round the oval shaped centre being made about that time. Some few efforts were also attempted to bring the place into popularity for residential purposes, but the malaria rising from the cultivated ground, (then paddifields), distributes its death-fever so liberally that the idea had to be abandoned. During more recent years the place has been scientifically drained and improved in many ways, and thereby divested of most of its poisonous atmosphere, so that to-day it forms the grandest Recreation-ground in this part of the world.

It is no uncommon thing of an afternoon, when the sun has dipped behind Victoria peak, to see from two to three thousand spectators anxiously watching some exciting contest at Football or Cricket. And at the Annual Race Meeting, which is held every year in the month of February, the numbers collected together will be ten times as great.

There is yet another interesting aspect in viewing this very beautiful spot. Many, very many, who have in their day been participants and eye-witnesses of the season's innocent sports and pastimes extending over a period in some few cases of nearly half a century; have finally taken up their last resting place in sight of their life's playground. There are four cemeteries on the hillside to the right hand of the valley. Taking them in the order of approach, they are the Mahommedan, Roman Catholic, Angelican, Parsee, and Hindoo, all beautiful as regards their monuments and the peaceful calm which surrounds them.

**The Central Market,** situated to the Westward about three minutes walk from the Clock Tower, is a very substantial brick and granite structure covering a large area and extending from the Queen's Road to the the Praya. Its upper story is confined to the supply of meat, poultry and fruit, including game when in season ; the basement being set apart for fish, vegetables and the use of wholesale dealers. The place is kept nice and clean and should be of interest to every visitor who may respect one of the most important of our sanitary and hygienic institutions.

# TWELVE TRIPS ON THE ISLAND.

## PROGRAMME No. 1.

### From the Peak via Pokfolum to the Clock Tower.

Leaving the Peak Tramway Station take the road to the left, when, on the right hand will be seen a well kept winding path leading down the hill.

In the distance the Maison de Nazareth, the Sanitorium de Bethanie and the Pokfolum Reservoir, with pretty slopes and mountain ridges and peaks in every direction, help to make up the view. The picture is full of interest. The beautiful sea studded with islands, the distant mountain range on Lantau with the far distant estuary of the Canton River; and, if the evening is chosen for the walk, a brilliant Sun-set will probably close the scene. On arriving at the bottom turn to the right past the Police station, the Douglas Castle and Santa Lucia. The road here is very pretty almost like a cliff walk with Mount Davis to the left. Many windings and a very gradual descent brings us within sight of two forts. Here, an extensive reclamation of the sea shore, also to our left, shows us the Rope works, the Silk Filature Factory and the Cattle depôt: keeping on past the forts, with a sudden turn to the right, some of the West-end residences, the City of Victoria with its harbour full of shipping, and the Kowloon peninsula in the distance. Continue on, still following to the same road, when half an hour later the R. C. Cathedral will appear in front of you. Take the turning to the left down the steps and you will in a few minutes reach the Clock Tower.

The 4 o'clock Tram is recommended for this trip.

## PROGRAMME No. 2.

### From the Peak via Magazine Gap to the Clock Tower.

Leaving the Peak Tramway Station take the road to the left proceeding by a gradual ascent over the hill, still continuing to keep to the left.

Here the views are charming. The mountain slopes covered with pine trees interspersed with rocky precipices and be-sprinkled with granite boulders. Mount Kellet on the right, the Port of Aberdeen in the valley with the beautiful open sea girt in by high-land in the far distance.

During the rainy season cataracts are visible in every direction, pouring down to contribute to make up the mountain torrent, which through the gully below, is hastening away to the sea.

The little English church is now visible, and beyond, a low gap opens up further lovely scenery, the summit of Mount Parker 5 miles away. Through this gap keep to the right, when at a short distance, a sharp turn to the left gets over the most intricate part of the route. The walk is now a delightful one. An easy road with much of interest on every hand. The wild flowers, the ferns, the variety of beautiful shrubs in bloom and the singing of the birds, contribute to show nature off to wonderful advantage. The varying hues of the foliage also help to give a finishing touch to the picture.

Half-an-hour over this charming hill road and the Magazine Gap with its umbrella seat is reached. Here turn to the left having the Harbour with its busy shipping and the central district of the City of Victoria in front of you. A gradual descent full of interest will in forty minutes find you on the lower levels, where by reference to the map or plan of the City, you will soon be able to select your route to the Clock Tower.

## PROGRAMME No. 3.

### From the Peak to the Clock Tower by the shortest route, the Peak Road.

On leaving the Peak Tramway Station turn sharp to the right following the road down the hill keeping always to the left. From the upper part of this road the views to the Eastward over the harbour, the Kowloon Peninsula and the mainland, are very fine; with the Ladies' Recreation Club, the Filter beds and the Bowen and Kennedy Roads in the foreground. In about 20 minutes the cross-roads will be reached, when by continuing straight forward, having the Public Gardens on either hand, the R. C. Cathedral will shortly be in sight. Here a turning to the right, down the steps, leads to the Clock Tower.

The afternoon is the best time to select for this trip as the road will be in the shade.

## PROGRAMME No. 4.

### From the Peak via Aberdeen and Pokfolum to the Clock Tower.

On leaving the Peak Tramway Station take the road to the left proceeding by a gradual ascent over the hill, when the views described in No. 2 will open up (the Port of Aberdeen in distance). Still keeping the road to the left, at a junction select the middle of three roads, which, in its zigzag windings will be seen to lead down the hill. The descent is rather abrupt so care should be taken not to hurry. The valley before us is exceedingly picturesque; the bold outline of Mount Kellet towering up on the right, and a forest of fir trees on every side, with a rear view including a number of charming Peak residences built as it were in every nook and cranny.

An easy walk with much happy variety brings us in about 40 minutes, to the main road below. Turning to the right past the high wall of the premises belonging to the Hongkong and Whampoa Dock Company, Limited, we have the entrance to the Port of Aberdeen, through a somewhat narrow strait, on our left.

A pretty stretch of sea-side continues until the bridge over a mountain stream, which we had also met with during the descent of the hill. At this point the road gradually rises until the model buildings of the Dairy Farm Company are visible. From here the walk is the same as in Programme No. 1 unless a desire to vary it suggests taking the path along the aquaduct which can be done, and will be seen a little above the road on the right hand side, some distance after having passed Douglas Castle. This aquaduct walk is a great favourite with those of the residents who know it. It is a beautiful shady path through endless patches of pine woods with sudden and unexpected glimpses of pretty scenery.

In about half an hour the filter beds of the Pokfolum Reservoir will be at hand, where a descent can be made on to the Bonham Road; or, by proceeding across the beds in a straight line from the approach, past the battery, and down a somewhat stoney water course, the high road on the Richmond Estate, the property of the Humphreys' Estate and Finance Company, Limited will be reached. From this point, continuing in the same direction, half an hour should find us at the Clock Tower.

## PROGRAMME No. 5.

### From the Peak via Aberdeen and the Wanchai Gap to the Clock Tower.

Proceed by exactly the same route as described in Programme No. 4, to Aberdeen, but on reaching the main road at the bottom of the hill, turn to the left, when about 50 yards in front of you, facing a stone bridge over a small canal, a pathway will be seen leading up the hill again. If time permits a short stroll through the quaint fishing village of Aberdeen will certainly interest,—but to return to the pathway, which at the beginning is somewhat trying in ascent, as again also at the end—a very delightful afternoon can be spent in a leisurely climb up this perfectly shaded road to the gap, which is visible at many points as you get higher. On reaching the top a turning will be seen on the left which takes you to Magasine Gap (Programme No. 2) but to continue—follow the road in front of you going at an easy pace until, in ten minutes, surrounded by interesting scenery, you reach the small service reservoir below, from which the aquaduct—Bowen Road, runs right and left. A few minutes further down the hill the Kennedy Road branches off, also to the left: either of these roads can be taken if the distance already covered has not proved too fatiguing, otherwise continue down the hill until you arrive at the Wanchai Road (leading to Queen's Road) where a ricksha can be hired to convey you to the Clock Tower.

## PROGRAMME No. 6

### From the Peak via Little Hongkong to Stanley.

Proceed exactly as in Programme No. 2 branching off by the hill path leading to the Military Sanitorium and following the course of a mountain stream until the road from Aberdeen to the Wanchai Gap is reached. Here turn to the left and in a few minutes a pathway will be visible on your right leading through a pine wood copse over a little knoll and down to the bed of a stream, with a reservoir a little distance, also to the right. Having rested to enjoy the pretty peaceful surroundings proceed very carefully to ascend the low hill on the opposite side of the stream.. This path leads through some very thick cover, is pretty well shaded and sometimes a little difficult to make out. In about 30 minutes you should discover the scent of burning wood with a faint blue smoke trying to find its escape from the now thickly grown forest. A little further on, the remains of the very primative village of Little Hongkong will come suddenly into view with a full chorus of dogs, pigs, and fowls. There is little to be seen here beyond a few relics of the past, in the shape of delapidated shanties with some curious specimens of the inhabitants and their children, generally clad in Nature's garb if the weather is not too cold.

Leaving the village, the main road is close by. To the right takes you to Aberdeen, and to the left, which is your direction, divides into three roads of which select the middle one keeping along by the sea shore. Here in a few minutes by a zigzag path you approach a stream, which having crossed, and having passed the shore station of the telegraph cable, the walk for some considerable distance becomes a little monotonous. The beautiful sea calmly reposing in many a pretty inlet. In 40 minutes, gradually ascending, the gap is reached from which point of elevation the Port of Stanley, situated on a narrow isthmus in a very picturesque little bay, can be seen to the very best advantage.

A steam-launch should be ready to convey you back to town as the journey is too great and too tiring to attempt to walk. However should you decide to try it, take the Stanley Road to Taitam (refer to Chart); a very interesting cliff and forest walk. The distance is about 9 miles.

## PROGRAMME No. 7.

### From the Clock Tower via Quarry Bay to Taitam.

Proceed by ricksha to the eastward as far as Bay View or Quarry Bay if you like ; the road not affording sufficient interest to recommend walking. Having passed the Entrance-lodge to the great Sugar Refinery, a pathway on the right just before crossing a bridge leads up the hill to a gap at an elevation of 1,000 feet, where the Sanitorium buildings for the use of the employees of the Sugar Refinery will be seen. The walk up this very easy gradient should be done without much exertion in about 50 minutes. At every turn of the road as you ascend, the scenery is interesting; the bold shoulders and entended spurs of Mount Parker particularly inviting for a climb. Above the bed of the water course on the left, where there are several small reservoirs, a wire-rope tramway will be seen, erected for the use also of the employees of the great Sugar Refinery. Having reached the top, after a few minutes rest to admire the beautiful surroundings, proceed leisurely down the zigzag path to the artificial lake, Taitam Reservoir, below.

This is the main water-supply of the Colony and, when full up to its overflow, is measured to contain about 400 millions of gallons.

The Catchment Area including that of the Catchwater Service exceeds 2,000 acres in extent. Having arrived at the dam from which the best views of the reservoir can be obtained, turn to the right round a little knoll, when a foot bridge crossing the overflow will lead to the main road for the return to town. A rather sharp ascent to the right finds us on a pleasant hill road amidst pretty undulations with an easy rise to another gap about a mile distant. Here a pause might be made to enjoy the ever changing scenery, and perhaps a beautiful sunset behind the distant peaks and ridges,—but, let us not forget that when the sun goes down in the tropics, darkness follows almost immediately, so that we should do well to reach the main road at the bottom of the hill. Proceeding on, at a sudden turn a short distance ahead, a cutting on the left discloses the road to Aberdeen via Little Hongkong; however, to keep to our programme a pleasant descent soon finds us in Happy Valley, at the further end of which a ricksha can be obtained to convey us back to the Clock Tower.

## PROGRAMME No. 8.

### From the Clock Tower via Shaukiwan to Taitam.

Proceed by ricksha or steam-launch *preferable* to the fishing village of Shaukiwan seven miles to the eastward close to the Lyemun Pass, *see map.*

On arriving in the main street, to the right of the market place, will be seen cut into a boulder, a steep pathway leading up the hill high above the left bank of a stoney watercourse, which it finally crosses and then joins a very distinguishable bridle road round the side of Mount Parker. Here the scenery is very pleasing. To the left the small sea-side village of Saiwan partly hidden by the foliage of lichee orchards. Above, a very narrow gap through which a splendid sea-view in the direction of Cape D'Aguilar with miles of rocky foreshore, is obtainable. To the right Mount Parker.

Proceeding on by a very easy ascent, at a sadden curve in the road we find ourselves in the upper gallery of an immence Amphi Theatre with continuous mountain ranges on every side. In the distance, well above the road, a line of masonry can be distinguished,—this is the Catch-water Service round Mount Parker for conserving the rainfall and conveying it to Taitam. By a short climb this catchwater can be reached and as the walking is good and almost level, half-an-hour will bring you to the reservoir.

But to keep to the programme,—follow the road round the Amphi Theatre until through a cutting on your right you discover a long zigzag descent with a pretty sheet of water, Taitam Harbour, in the distance. Follow this pathway until a lengthy curve to the right brings the village of Taitam Tuk, with its exceedingly picturesque surroundings, into view. The inhabitants here are very primative and the children generally very inquisitive. Pass through the village over a white bridge to the left and take the road to the right over a second *stone* bridge. Here the scenery is on every hand very charming. Mountain, hill, and dale, valley, and ravine, with *such* a brook, or, in the rainy season, mountain torrent, as is not to be met with anywhere else on the island. This is also the most thickly wooded locality with forests of fir trees, wild azaleas and many other flowering shrubs and creepers. Orchids are also to be found near at hand.

From this point a very steep ascent brings us to the level of the overflow from the reservoir, with its bridge on our left hand. The trip from here to the Clock Tower may be undertaken in two ways as described in Programme No. 7.

## PROGRAMME No. 9.

### From the Clock Tower along the Bowen Road to Happy Valley.

*To do this walk thoroughly a start should be made not later than 4 o'clock.*

Poceed up Wyndham Street which ascends the hill almost facing the entrance to the Clock Tower. In a few minutes you have the depôt of the Dairy Farm on your left, cross over the road and continue up the hill entering the Public Gardens with the Roman Catholic Cathedral on your right; keep straight on by the side of a nullah until you reach the road at the top having a stone bridge, also on your right. Here turn to the left and in a few minutes cross-roads are again reached; keep the same direction past the rear of a terrace of houses when you will see by a curve to the right the embankment of the filter beds, and, a short distance beyond, the commencement of the aquaduct or Bowen Road. You have now a delightful walk, practically level, of about four miles.

To do this walk is to know something of the pleasures of life on this island. There is not a finer promenade to be found any where than that of the Bowen Road, Hongkong.

The scenery is magnificent at all points with such endless variety as to entirely preclude the possibility of fatigue. Having arrived at the entrance to the tunnel which is approached after crossing a hill-road, a rest for a few minutes will prove enjoyable.

Here the view towards the valley is one of the finest of the many of which this Island can boast. The Recreation Ground with its race course, grand stand and stables; the China Sugar Refinery with Morrison Hill on the left, the Man-of-war anchorage, Kowloon Peninsula and a mountain range, with the stately peak of Tai-mo-shan standing out above all others, on the Mainland in the distance. However, it is time to move and, for those who may be too tired, rickshas can be obtained at the other end of the recreation ground, about 20 minutes distant—although the proper thing is to retrace one's steps, as the views are much finer on the return trip, with the possibility of an interesting sun-set.

The Bowen Road affords perhaps the best opportunity for getting a favorable impression of the many advantages in which this Colony outrivals other colonies. With its scenery, its water, and its walk, and its absolutely pure mountain atmosphere, assuredly it should have no competitors.

## PROGRAMME No. 10.

### From the Clock Tower via Kennedy Road to Happy Valley.

Proceed along Queen's Road until opposite the New Victoria Hotel, when by the way of Battery-path, leading up to the Old Murray Battery constructed in the year 1845, turning suddenly to the right with the Government Offices on your left, you will notice a rather steep pathway in front of you protected by an iron railing on a granite support. This pathway takes you up a few stone steps on to the main road with Government House grounds on your right. In a few minutes you have the principal entrance to the Public Gardens in view. Here turn to the left and a pretty ornamental granite bridge at once introduces Kennedy Road. This is a short but very pleasant walk, one of the earliest, as a fashionable resort, attempted along the side of the hill. Having passed the first decided bend, at a distance of some two hundred yards, a seat will be found where a magnificent view of the Peak, the upper residences (Queen's Gardens) Government House, the Portestant Cathedral, the City Hall, and in fact a landscape composed of nearly all the principal European residences with the ever present harbour and mainland in the distance. Half-an-hour can be well spent here admiring these beautiful surroundings, which by a glance at the Historical Sketch, *pages 1 to 40*, will provide food for reflection.

To think that in less than three score years, within the memory of thousands living at the present day, all that you now behold has been invented, developed and accomplished by that spirit of sheer determination, generating a multitude of race forces, which have one and all in a greater or lesser degree, contributed to such a wonderful completion.

To proceed,—keeping on about the same level after several windings a big granite boulder occupies the centre of the road and the Naval Hospital can be seen pleasantly situated on a low hill to the left. Here the Kennedy Road walk may be considered as ended for those who do not care to continue on to the valley. But for those who prefer to complete the programme, follow on in the same direction when a deep dip into the hills, past a very steep mountain-road on your right finally brings you after a long curve to the Wanchai Road with a little Wesleyan Chapel on your left. Here turn to the right and a deep cutting through the hill with a gradual descent brings you to the Happy Valley. A walk round this lovely spot or into one or more of the cemeteries will occupy an hour when a ricksha can be found near the Golf Club Pavilion which will convey you in about ten minutes back to the Clock Tower.

## PROGRAMME No. 11,

### From the Clock Tower via Wong-nei-cheong and Taitam to Quarry Bay.

As this is rather a long trip, an early start, not later than 3 o'clock should be made by ricksha to the extreme end of Happy Valley where at the left hand corner the road leads up the hill.

An easy ascent, the surroundings are at once interesting. The scattered village of Wong-nei-cheong with its wonderful little terraces of cultivation, not an inch of ground wasted; and its primative system of irrigation making the very best use possible of its limited water supply. Having crossed a wooden bridge the road bears to the right becoming a little more steep, until the Bowen Road is reached also on your right, and on your left a cutting leads to this end of the aquaduct tunnel, fifty yards distant.

The views from the embankment here are very extensive. Taking to the road again, the walk is very pleasant until on your right another cutting points the direction to Little Hongkong and Aberdeen. Immediately beyond, a curve to the left places you on a ridge, and for a few minutes the gradient becomes perceptibly steeper, the scenery continuing to improve all the time.

Now a short curve to the right followed by one to the left and the gap appears just ahead. This is the highest point in the road, and a very easy descent through pretty hill country soon brings you in sight of the great reservoir at Taitam. Here some time can be spent, and as the exit-end of the tunnel was inspected on the other side of the hill, about one and a half mile distant; the entrance-end, which can be seen from the dam, might also be visited.

This is perhaps the grandest piece of engineering work that has ever been attempted in this part of the world. The dam, although simple enough in conception, is an immense piece of solid masonry, and then the outlet from the dam to the aquaduct is equally wonderful.

Having satisfied ourselves with a rest and what we have seen, the ascent of the hill in the direction of the Sanitorium should be commenced. This will take about half-an-hour, and when at the top, another rest, with the views to the North as well as to the South, will occupy a few minutes. Then follows a very pleasant down-hill walk with another gigantic piece of engineering work in the distance at the bottom of the hill. This is the great Sugar Refinery, one of the largest in the world. Arrived at the bottom, at a little distance to the left, rickshas can generally be found which will convey you to the Clock Tower, *5 miles distant* in about 40 minutes.

## PROGRAMME No. 12.

### Kowloon (Nine Dragons).

That portion of the British Crown Colony of Hongkong known as Kowloon comprises part of the peninsula which stretches into the harbour from the mainland on the North. It contains about three square miles of barren hill country and was ceded to the British in the year 1861.

Prior to this cession, its position had long been a considerable menace and annoyance to the rising young Colony, for it served as a handy place of rendezvous, so to speak, for all the lawless rabble from the neighbouring districts, who lived by smuggling, plundering and harassing the honest trader, at the same time taking good care to keep outside the jurisdiction of the Colonial Government.

In its earlier history, Kowloon has also been the battle ground of many a feud and faction fight between the Puntis and the Hakkas, and to this very day is to be seen close to the boundry line, an inscription on a granite boulder. denoting the place of final surrender of the last of the Taipings in the neighbourhood.

During the 35 years of the British occupation, improvements equally as great as those on the Island of Hongkong have been the natural following.

Good roads in every direction. The foreshore extensively reclaimed, with Docks, Wharves and Godowns and where a convenient water frontage was necessary, many other industries have sprung up.

An important military camp with roomy barracks is another prominent feature and is at present occupied by an Indian native regiment. An observatory, ably performing its scientific functions, added to which numerous very pretty residences detached and in terraces are to be seen conveniently situated, overlooking the harbour.

On the Western shore of this peninsula is the Port or village of Yaumati, a little Capital in itself, with its shipping returns, fishing and boat building industries, a fine market place, and gas and water laid on complete. The Chinese at Yaumati are distinct from those resident in Hongkong. Their shops are cleaner and different in style, with a variety of curious little wares not to be met with across the water.

It is a pleasant afternoon's outing to take the 3 o'clock launch, and a ricksha on leaving the wharf at Kowloon with the order 'for Yaumati' (20 minutes) walking through the principal street, and then by ricksha again through the hills to Hung-ham where the gigantic establishment of the Hongkong and Whampoa Dock Company Limited is to be seen.

The streets in Hung-ham, are also fine and wide, and there is another extensive market place, with a curious agglomeration of shanties on the sea shore occupied chiefly by the employees of the native boat builders and their families.

On leaving Hung-ham take the ricksha once more, keeping to the bund the whole distance, past the coal godowns of Messrs. Blackhead & Co. on your left, round the Chim-sa-choi point, having the handsome building of the Water Police Station always on your right, and in less than half-an-hour you should reach the ferry-launch opposite to the main entrance to the Wharf and Godown Company's premises, when ten minutes will land you in Hongkong.

There is a little food for reflection in what you have seen during your two hours trip, when you come to think that Kowloon as a British possession is only 35 years old, and that even up to within the last fifteen years the place had, with the exception of the Docks, remained in an almost dormant state, owing in some measure to its being considered unhealthy. Kowloon has yet to play its most important role. At some future time it will undoubtedly provide the site of terminus for the extensive railway system which, when it comes, will be the regenerating power of this part of the neighbouring Empire. May *we* all live to see it.

# A FONG'S Views of Hongkong, &c.

No.                    Description.

1.—Sampans.
2.—A Chinese Street.
3.—         do.
4.—         do.
5.—The Praya looking, East.
6.—         do.         do.  West.
7.—The Cemeteries, Happy Valley.
8.—The City of Victoria and Harbour.
9.—         do.         do.         do.
10.—The Peak Tramway.
11.—The Public Gardens.
12.—The Government House.
13,—             do.
14.—Cargo Junks.
15.—The Peak Residences.
16.—    do.         do.
17.—The Hongkong Hotel.
18.—The Hongkong and Shanghai Bank.
19.—Means of Conveyance.
20 —The Race Course, Happy Valley.
21.—The Joss House, Happy Valley.
22.—The Queen's Road Central.
23.—The Tramway Station.
24.—The Queen's Road.

NOTE.—*The above views from a representative series, but there are*
*a great many more to select from including views of the Coast Ports.*

A FONG,
*Ice House Street.*

# A FONG'S Views of Canton, Peking, &c.

*No.*              *Description.*

25.—The Canton River.

26.—A Mandarin's Grave.

27.—A Street in Canton.

28.—The Flowery Pagoda.

29.—A Flower Boat.

30.—A Chinese Garden.

31.—The Temple of 500 Genii.

32.—The Examination Hall.

33.—The Reception Room Howqua's Residence.

34.—Guardians of the Portals, Honam Temple.

35.—The Dragon Festival.

36.—The Five Storey Pagoda.

## PEKING.

37.—The Imperial Palace.

38.—           do.

39.—A Street in Peking.

40.—The Dragon Throne, Peking.

41.—The Observatory, Peking.

42.—The Ming Tombs.

43.—A Marriage Procession.

44.—A Funeral.

45.—Coolies in their " Rain Coats."

46.—A Fortune Teller.

47.—Li King Ching and Suite.

48.—Female Small Foot.

NOTE.—*The above views from a representative series, but there are a great many more to select from including views of the Coast Ports.*

A FONG,

*Ice House Street.*

# Humphreys' Estate and Finance Co., Ld.

AUTHORISED CAPITAL... ... ... ... ... $ 1,000,000.
SUBSCRIBED ,, ... ... ... ... ... 254,000.
RESERVE FUND ... ... ... ... ... ... 30,000.

## THE ESTATE INCLUDES

THE RICHMOND ESTATE. THE KOWLOON ESTATE.

ROAD FRONTAGE...3,760 FT. ROAD FRONTAGE...6,470 FT.
AREA...............386,700 SQ. FT. AREA...............536,300 SQ. FT.

*See annexed plans.*

### GOVERNING DIRECTORS:

## JOHN D. HUMPHREYS & SON.

### BANKERS:

## THE HONGKONG & SHANGHAI BANKING CORPORATION.

THIS COMPANY is prepared to act as Special Agents or Attorneys, Liquidators, Executors or Administrators; as Trustees, House and Estate Agents for Residents or Non-residents, and, on commission, to buy or sell Property, to advance money against Mortgage, to invest funds in Mortgage or otherwise, to buy or sell Shares or local stocks, and generally to act for those who may be temporarily or permanently absent from the Colony.

### OFFICES:

## 38 & 40, Queen's Road Central.

# INFORMATION.

**THE HIRE** of steam-launch, Hakka boat or sampan for Deep Bay or Mirs Bay is by special arrangement for the trip.

Say from Saturday afternoon until Sunday night or early Monday morning.

According to the size of launch...$18.00 to $24.00

According to the size of Hakka boat ........................ } $ 8.00 to $12.00

Sampan ..............................$ 2.00 to $ 3.00

Native boats or punts ...........$ 1.00 per day.

Hongkong coolies (chow allowance included) ....... } $ 1.00 ,,

There is an advantage in taking Hongkong coolies, as the natives are very independent and sometimes even impudent.

Where village boys are employed to carry ammunition and to retrieve, 20 cents per day is usual with a cumshow according to the bag, but anything that may be entrusted to their care should most certainly be under lock and key.

## TIDES.

As space will not admit of a daily tide table, the few remarks below may be useful, with the recommendation to obtain a copy of the tide tables for Singapore and Hongkong from the Harbour Office, price 50 cents.

**NOTE:**—Owing to the numerous passages though the many islands, especially to the westward of Hongkong, the tides or tidal currents are at times not to be relied on and local experience in such cases becomes invaluable. As a rule it will be found safe to leave for Deep Bay on the first of the flood, or say at dead low water in Hongkong.

R. C. H.

# EIGHT SHORT TRIPS TO THE MAINLAND.

## INTRODUCTION.

These short trips to the Mainland are more especially intended for gentlemen in robust health, who, having time at their disposal and perhaps a liking for sport, are prepared to rough it in a measure, sleeping on board a steam-launch or native boat, or in a Joss house for as many nights as the party made decide to remain away. Such an experiment would at first sight seem a folly, but to the local *shikari*, there is untold pleasure in these outings,— besides, a 20 mile tramp across hill country is, in this part of the world, considered to be by far and away the best medicine for resuscitating the over taxed senses.

The subjoined map describes the most southern portion of the Sun On District situated in that part of the Kwangtung Province immediately adjacent to the British Crown Colony of Hongkong. The object with which it has been compiled is to encourage and assist the Hongkong resident, as well as the tourist, to become acquainted with a neighbourhood or district that, at no far distant date may assume a position of special interest and show unmistakable signs of a very rapid development.

Although on a first glance the landscape appears to be composed of little else than barren hills plentifully besprinkled with black looking objects, which on closer examination prove to be weather-beaten, sun-burnt granite boulders, yet behind these ranges of hills there are many thousands of acres of rich valley land where fruit, rice and a variety of other cereals and tubers are extensively cultivated. Besides these, sugar cane, ground nut and sweet potatoes thrive on the lower slopes, and patches of them may occasionally be seen on portions of rising ground surrounded by the flooded paddy fields. Garden fruit and vegetables of the usual varieties are also to be met with in the larger villages, about the confines of which, they are cultivated mostly for home consumption.

In the neighbourhood of Deep Bay, more particularly to the eastward, the lichee is abundantly grown, and in the Bay itself will be found the most extensive oyster beds in this part of the province. This locality also provides the hunting ground for local Sportsmen.

Commencing from about the middle of August, snipe abound throughout the valleys, six weeks later quail begin to appear on the stubble and, with the assistance of a dog, partridges may be found on the hill sides as also a few pheasants in the thicker cover. Throughout the winter waterfowl, including the blue heron, are plentiful in great variety, especially in the creeks and on the mud flats of the bay, with shell pigeons and ring-doves in the bamboo groves which generally surround the villages. In the district covered by this map, there are many enjoyable trips both for the pedestrian and the sportsman; and the author, soliciting every consideration for shortcomings, trusts that the following pages will prove both useful and interesting to those who may have the leisure to peruse them.

HONGKONG, April 1897.

# OUTFIT NECESSARY.

---

As the trips will not as a rule exceed two or perhaps three days, no great preparation need be made as if for a lengthened stay.

Passports (*always useful*) *procurable through your Consul in Canton:* and the national flag of the party.

Boat.—Steam-launch and, or, Hakka-boat with a small punt or dingy.

Wardrobe.—Seasonable, according to duration of trip (sun topey indispensible *flannels recommended*.)

Commissariat.—Fresh water, fresh meat, pies, bread, potatoes, salt, tinned meats, butter, milk and preserves, tea, coffee, sugar, and a cruet.

Light.—Oil lamps, candles, *matches*.

Sporting gear.—Tiger rifle, fowling piece, duck gun and revolver, with *ammunition* for all.

Recreation.—Cards, reading matter, cigars and tobacco.

Personal.—Medicines and Liquors.

Pocket *Compass and pedometer:*

# VOCABULARY
## (IN CANTONESE AND HAKKA).

NOTE.—You are advised to show the characters in preference to any attempt to pronounce them, as the right tones are difficult to give and a very slight error in *tone* may alter the meaning of the word.

| | CANTONESE. | | HAKKA. |
|---|---|---|---|
| Yes!............ ...... | Hai ............ ...... | 係 | Hay. |
| No! ...... ........ .... | Mò ...... ........ .... | 冇 | Maú. |
| Cash ............. ....... | Ts'in ............. ...... | 錢 | Ts'en. |
| Dollars ........... | Ngan ............ ...... | 銀 | Nyoon. |
| No. 1 ............ ........ | Yat ...... ........ .. | 壹 | Yeet. |
| 2............ ...... | I ............ ...... | 弍 | Ngee. |
| 3............. ...... | Sàm ............ ..... | 叁 | Sahm. |
| 4............. ...... | Si ............ ...... | 肆 | See. |
| 5............ ...... | Ng ............ ...... | 伍 | Ng. |
| 6............ .. | Luk ........ ....... | 陸 | Look. |
| 7............. ...... | Ts'at ............ .. | 柒 | Ts'eet. |
| 8............. ...... | Pàt. ........ ....... | 捌 | Paht. |
| 9............. ...... | Kau ............ ...... | 玖 | Keeoo. |
| 10............. ...... | Shap ............ .... | 拾 | Sheep. |
| 11............. ...... | Shap-yat .......... | 十一 | Sheep-yeet. |
| 12............. ...... | Shap-i ............ | 十二 | Sheep-ngee. |
| 20............. ...... | I-shap ........ .. | 二十 | Ngee-sheep. |
| 30............. ...... | Sàm-shap ...... | 三十 | Sahm-sheep. |
| 40...... ........ | Si-shap ........... | 四十 | See-sheep. |
| 50............. ...... | Ng-shap .......... | 五十 | Ng-sheep. |

| | CANTONESE. | | HAKKA. |
|---|---|---|---|
| 100 | Yat-pák | 一佰 | Yeet pahk. |
| 1,000 | Yat-ts'in | 一千 | Yeet-ts'en. |
| 10,000 | Yat-mán | 一萬 | Yeet-wahn. |
| Immediately | Tsik hák | 即刻 | Tsit kheat. |
| By and by | Chi 'há | 遲吓 | Mahn-mahn-tsz. |
| Many thanks | To tsé | 多謝 | To tsea. |
| Wait a little | Tang há | 等吓 | Then ha. |
| I want something to eat | Ngo iú shik yé | 我要食野 | Ngai oi shit tung-se. |
| Please bring me | To fán ním pi ngo | 多煩拈俾我 | To fan cha pun ngai. |
| Rice | Fán | 飯 | Me. |
| Bread | Min páu | 麵飽 | Men-pow. |
| Meat (beef) | Ngau yuk | 凍牛肉 | Nyook. |
| Fowl | Kai hong | 鷄項 | Kigh ts'ai. |
| Fish | Shang ü | 生魚 | Ng. |
| Oysters | Hò | 蠔 | Hò |
| Eggs | Kai tán | 鷄旦 | Kigh ch'oon. |
| Biscuits | Peng kon | 餅干 | Peng kon. |
| Oranges | Kom ch'áng | 橙 | Kahm. |
| Bananas | Héung ngá tsiú | 香芽蕉 | Heong ts'yow. |
| Tea | Ch'á | 茶 | Ts'ah. |
| Sugar | Pák t'ong | 白糖 | T'ong. |
| Wine | 'Tsau | 酒 | Tseeoo. |
| Salt | Sháng ím | 生鹽 | Yahm. |
| Knife | Yat chéung tò tsai | 一張刀仔 | Tow. |
| Fork | Yat chi ch'á | 一枝义 | Ts'ah. |
| Spoon | Shi kang | 匙羹 | Chee kahng. |

| | CANTONESE. | | HAKKA. |
|---|---|---|---|
| Water | Shui | 水 | Shooee. |
| Hot Water | It shui | 熱水 | Show shooee. |
| Cold Water | Tung shui | 凍水 | Lahng shooee. |
| It is unnecessary | M' shai | 唔使 | M' sz. |
| Be careful | Siú sam | 小心 | Seaú sim. |
| That will do | Ni ko tsò tak | 呢個做得 | Tso tet. |
| Good morning | Tsò shan | 早晨 | Ts'au shin. |
| I want to buy (something) | Ngo iú mái tik yé | 我要買的野 | Ngai oi mai tung se. |
| Sweet potatoes | Fán shü | 蕃薯 | Fan shue. |
| Oil | Yau | 油 | Yiu. |
| Kerosine | Fo shui | 火水 | Fo shui. |
| Matches | Fo ch'ai | 火柴 | Fo ts'ai. |
| Rope | Shing | 繩 | Shin. |
| Bamboos | Chuk | 竹 | Chuk. |
| Capons | Shin kai | 善鷄 | Yam kai. |
| Turkey | 'Fo kai | 火鷄 | Fo kai. |
| Vegetables | Ts'oi | 菜 | T'soi. |
| Spinach | In ts'oi | 莧菜 | Hean t'soi. |
| Lettuce | Shang ts'oi | 生菜 | Shang tsoi. |
| Pamelloes | Luk yau | 碌柚 | Luk. |
| What is the price? | Ki to ká ts'in | 幾多價錢 | Ke to ka tsen. |
| Too dear | Tái kwai | 太貴 | Tai kwei. |
| Will you take less? | Kám siú tik | 減少的 | Kam shaú taeu. |
| I am satisfied | Tsau kòm lok | 就叫咯 | Kan tso tet. |
| Be quick | Fái tik | 快的 | Fai te. |
| This is mine | Hai ngo ké | 係我嘅 | Hea nga kai. |

| | CANTONESE. | | HAKKA. |
|---|---|---|---|
| Put in paper | Pí chí pán hò | 俾紙包好 | Pun che paú haú |
| Pack it up in wood case | Pí séung chong hò | 俾箱庄好 | Pun seong ch'ong haú. |
| That will do | Tsò tak | 做得 | Tso tek |
| I must go | Ngo teng iú hü | 我定要去 | Ngai tin oi hé. |
| See my Passport | Im' ngo fong' hang 'chi | 驗我放行紙 | Neam ngai kai fong hang che |
| I am | Ngo hai | 我係 | Ngai Hae. |
| English | Yíng kwok yan | 英國人 | Yin keak nyin. |
| French | Fát kwok yan | 法國人 | Fat keak nyin. |
| German | Tak kwok yan | 德國人 | Tet keak nyin. |
| American | Fá k'i yan | 花旗人 | Fa khi keak nyin. |
| Portuguese | Sai yéung yan | 西洋人 | Si yeong keak nyin. |
| Take me to | Tai ngo hü | 帶我去 | Tai ngai he. |
| A mandarin | Kún fú | 官府 | Kon fu. |
| The Teepo | Ti' 'pò | 地保 | Ti paú. |
| The sea shore | Hoi 'pin | 海邊 | Hoi pen. |
| The river bank | Ho 'pin | 河邊 | Ho pen. |
| The boat | Siú 't'eng | 小艇 | Seau theang. |
| The missionary | Ch'ün káu yan | 傳教人 | Tsin Kaú nyin. |
| The village | Ts'ün h'eung | 村鄉 | Tsún heong. |
| The others | Pit tik | 別的 | Phet ngee sa. |
| Go with me | T'ung ngo hü | 仝我去 | Lau ngai he. |
| Do not trouble me | Mat wan ngo | 勿運我 | M' ho kaú ngai. |
| I do not require you | Ngo m shai ni | 我唔使你 | Ngai m' sz ngee |
| Do not hurt me | Mat tá ngo | 勿打我 | M' haú ta ngai. |
| Be patient | Yan noi | 忍耐 | Nyun nai. |
| I beg pardon | M koi | 唔該 | M' koi. |

| | CANTONESE. | | HAKKA. |
|---|---|---|---|
| He did it on purpose | K'ü tak í tsò | 佢特意做 | Khe ku yee cho. |
| What is that to you? | U ni ho kon | 於你何干 | Kwan ngee mak kai sz. |
| Good-bye | Hò hang lái | 好行拉 | Hau hang. |
| Come and see me | Loi kin ngo | 來見我 | Loi ken ngai. |
| What time is it? | Ki tím chung | 幾點鐘 | Ke tó tem chung. |
| Five o'clock | Ng tím chung | 五點鐘 | Ng tem chung. |
| Half past six | Luk tím pún | 六點半 | Luk tem pan chung. |
| What place is this? | Hai mat yé tí fong | 係乜野地方 | Hea mak kai te fong. |
| I am going ashore | Ngo shéung ngon | 我上岸 | Ngai sheong ngan. |
| Is there game here? | Ní ch'ü yau tséuk (tā mòu) | 呢處有雀 | Neha yin yew teow (tshi mau'.) |
| Pheasants | Shán kai | 山鷄 | San kai. |
| Partridges | Ché kú | 鷓鴣 | Cha ku. |
| Quail | Om shun | 鵪鶉 | Am shun. |
| Snipe | Shá chui | 沙逳 | Sha chui. |
| Teal | Shui áp | 水鴨 | Shuey ap. |
| Duck | Tái áp | 大鴨 | Ap. |
| Wild pig | Shán chü | 山猪 | San chu. |
| Goose | Ngo | 鵝 | Ngo. |
| Tiger | Lò fú | 老虎 | Lau fo. |
| Leopard | Páu | 豹 | Pau. |
| Deer | Luk | 鹿 | Luk. |
| Show me where they are | Wá ngo chi hai pín chü | 話我知係邊處 | Wa ngai te choi nai li. |
| Carry this | Nim ni tik yé | 拈呢的野 | Cha ngea teow he. |
| Be very careful | Siú sam tik | 小心的 | Seaú sim. |

| | CANTONESE. | | HAKKA. |
|---|---|---|---|
| Take me to the boat | Tüng ngo lok shün | 仝我落船 | Tai ngai lok shun. |
| Come again at | Tsoi loi kwo | 再來過 | Tsai loi. |
| To-morrow morning | Ming ch'iú tsó | 明朝早 | Nim chaú Tsaú. |
| I will reward you | (Ngo) shéung ni | 賞你 | Ta sheong ngee. |
| Heave up anchor | Hí náu p'ò | 起鐃泡 | Kau naú. |
| Hurry away | Hang fái tik | 行快的 | Hang fai te. |

# EIGHT TRIPS ON THE MAINLAND.

## PROGRAMME No. 1.

### To Tsin Wan and return via Kowloon Gap and City.

Proceed by launch or boat to Tsin-Wan—or, should you wish to shorten the distance—to Cheang Sha Wan.

From Tsin-Wan you steer in an easterly direction keeping to the valley paths all the time, and in less than an hour the village of Skek-li-pui, very prettily situated amongst the hills, will be reached. A little rest, and half an hour more brings you to the open where the village of Kang-hau will be seen on the right of some extensive paddy fields, the blue waters of Mirs Bay and the White Head, a small promontory jutting out into the Bay, in the distance.

Should you prefer to try the Cheung-Sha-Wan route, a twenty minutes climb passing the Custom's Station (matshed) brings you to the ridge from which a magnificent view over Kowloon peninsula with the Island and Harbour of Hongkong to the south, is before you. Your direction from the ridge is to the right, taking either the highest or middle path, the former cannot be mistaken as it leads round the upper shoulders of the range until a gap, just under the Lion's Head, is reached, where will be seen a small white house also a Custom's look-out station.

From this point the route is very plain as you can either approach Kowloon direct or continue the path round the hills until the stone road leading up from Kang-hau to the gap is joined.

If the middle path be selected one hour's walk through pretty *rough* hill country brings you to the

open, a long trip of paddy just under the Pinacle Rock
to the south from which long strip passing through a
very pretty bit of woodded scenery you arrive at the
same extensive paddy cultivation with the village of Kang-
hau on your right. From this point there is a good
stone road leading straight up the hill which is joined
by the path round the shoulders of the range at an
elevation of nearly 1,000 feet; — or, to take the easiest and
most frequented route, keep to the valley proceeding
eastward until having passed a large square white
building (the local house of refuge in case of an attack
by pirates or rebels) you will discover a much worn
stone road nearly facing you and leading up to the well
defined Kowloon Gap on your right. As all the routes
described converge to this gap it is here advisable to
make a lengthened halt after such a tedious ascent. The
view from this point is very fine, somewhat similar to
the one described from Cheung-Sha-Wan.

The Kowloon native city with its wall and square
built pawn shops lies in the valley a little to the right, and
in its apparent nearness, is very deceiving as it will
take a good hour to reach and a further good hour to
get to the launch at Kowloon Wharf.

## PROGRAMME No. 2.

### To Castle Peak and return via Un-tan Gap.

Note.—When the passage of the Cap-Siu-Moon
pass is contemplated it would be as well to consult the
tide table ; as, to attempt such passage in a Hakka boat
on an ebb tide without the aid of a steam-launch would
prove a very patience trying job.

Proceed to Castle Peak and on leaving the boat,
give instructions as to her destination. If very early
in the season land on the right hand side of the bay,

(if later, say October, the left hand side might be used as there are generally quail to be got within a few yards of the shore) taking the route as starred in the map, passing the village of San-Hu-Wai, immediately beyond which, snipe will be found in the paddy fields and on the marshes. The bed of a stream here sometimes proves useful for waterfowl and a little further on a small lagoon has been known to yield well, even to the blue heron. If the weather is not too hot and a full day is decided upon, proceed rapidly taking just the cream of the sport until the market village of Piang Shan is reached, thence across a low sort of gap where the range of hills on the right has all but fallen away. This leads into the Shap-pat-Heung valley where turn to the right and follow the red starred route, shooting at leisure, to the foot of the hills, taking a neat little pass which will be plainly visible. This pass lands us at the village of Un-tan where, according to the instructions given to the Hakka boat, we can proceed to Tai-Lam-Chung, or by the much shorter route to the village at the back of the island of Ma-wan, in the Cap-Siu-Moon pass, thence to Hongkong in a couple of hours, according to tide.

---

## PROGRAMME No. 3.

### To Tai Mo Shan and return via Lam-Fong-To.

This is, properly speaking, a picnic trip, and perhaps the most enjoyable one out of Hongkong. Have an early breakfast and leave by steam-launch for Tsin Wan, about one hours' steaming—land by native boat in the bay and proceed through the village or on the embankment. It is a good plan to hire a village lad as a guide, who will also assist in carrying the tiffin basket, always keeping *him* on ahead. The walk is a pretty one for some distance until the ascent begins, which at first is somewhat abrupt, but afterwards for several miles the road is good and of an easy gradient. When about half the way up you leave the main path for a sort of coolie track on the right, thereby making straight for what appears to be the summit. An hours steady climb will undeceive you, as you will suddenly discover a further height apparently only a few hundred yards above. This is the final summit, having a little flat top about one acre in extent. The elevation here is nearly 1,200 feet above anything in the immediate neighbourhood, hence the view in all directions is unsurpassed. Tiffin should now be partaken of and after an hours' rest the descent may be commenced down the eastern slope of the hill through the village of Lam-Fong-To until the rocky bed of a stream is reached with several pretty cataracts as we proceed. We are soon again amongst the patches of cultivated soil on the hill sides, and shortly find ourselves in Tsin Wan, where, if time permits, some native industries may be inspected. A *dip* from the launch if the water is not too cold will prove refreshing before steaming away for Hongkong.

## PROGRAMME No. 4.

### To Deep Bay and return via Castle Peak.

Proceed over night to Deep Bay by steam-launch accompanied by a sampan and a small punt or dingy. Instruct steam-launch as to destination. Land at day break on the southern shore as near as possible to the village of San-Wai which is situated close to a low hill and is well shaded by banyan trees. The very extensive paddy fields in this neighbourhood afford excellent cover for snipe, which in the early season are abundantly plentiful. Follow the beaten track skirting the many villages, direction almost due south, and with shooting all the way, you will, in a few hours, find yourself on the shores of Castle Peak Bay where your steam-launch should be in readiness to convey you back to Hongkong.

## PROGRAMME No. 5.

### To Deep Bay and return via Ma-On-Kong and the Telegraph pass.

This is one of the longest and most important trips and should not be undertaken unless one is thoroughly *fit.*

Proceed by steam-launch, or having due regard to the tide, by Hakka boat accompanied by sampan, to Deep Bay, approaching as near to the head of the bay as soundings will allow. Rise at daybreak and after a substantial meal and the necessary arrangements for a like substantial tiffin to be consumed *en route* land from the sampan at the head of the first creek in the river on your right, about one mile from the entrance. Shooting begins immediately with water fowl, curlew, plover, duck, teal, and sometimes geese. Snipe are always to be found from August until March, and spring snipe even later. Having secured the quantum of such as the river, marshes and paddy fields have to offer, you must now strike inland, making for the nearest village, Maipo, where you may, if the season is well advanced add a few pigeons to the bag. From this point the *tramp* begins, skirting the base of the hills on our left and passing from village to village giving to each a modicum of our time and attention. About 10 o'clock should bring us to the ancient walled market town of Kam-Tin-Ho, a very formidable looking place, well situated in the centre of an extensive and beautiful valley. Here a halt might be called for half an hour. From this point we proceed leisurely so as to tiffin at Ma-On-Kong which place we leave at 3 o'clock following the telegraph wires over the hills, until about 5.30 should find us in Tsin Wan, one hour from Hongkong by steam launch. A *dip* if there is time completes the trip.

## PROGRAMME No. 6.

### To Deep Bay return via Pat-Heung and Tai-Mo-Shan pass.

This trip is only a slight deviation from the last (Programme No. 5), as we proceed over exactly the same country up to the walled market town of Kam-Tin-Ho. From this point we strike off to the eastward, rounding another group of low hills in the Pat-Heung valley, before facing the Tai-Mo-Shan pass. In this neighbourhood partridges are reported to be very plentiful especially on the rising ground to the left of the approach to the road leading up the hill. The country here is certainly interesting and probably contains unknown treasure both for the sportsman as also for the explorer. We must not lose too much time as it will take at least three hours to cross the mountain to Tsin-Wan where our boat should be in waiting for us.

## PROGRAMME No. 7.

### To Deep Bay, Black Rock, Shatau, Shek-ha and Sham-chun.

This trip should occupy at least two days as it covers a line of country which will be found specially interesting. Proceed by steam-launch or Hakka boat accompanied by sampan, to Deep Bay, and if possible, anchor within a mile of Black Rock, an isolated granite boulder situated at a slight elevation on the northern shore of the Bay. Having partaken of a hearty breakfast and made the necessary arrangements for tiffin, *departure* rendezvous, &c., get ashore and strike inland, when, at a short distance you will perceive a clump of trees with one specially large banyan tree in the fore-front. Immediately in the neighbourhood of these trees is a bit of marshy ground overgrown with rushes where snipe in particular abound. This patch should occupy the attention of several guns for some time. The direction is now easterly along the shore of the bay until around Sha-Tao there are many such corners of interest including two small lagoons.. Continuing on to Shekkha we have to pass quite a number of villages surrounded by plantations of lichee trees and bamboo canes. Pigeons here are very plentiful and remain so in the shooting from village to village all the way up to the market twon of Sham-Chun. As it is not proposed to go further than this market town, to retrace our steps we can decide upon either bank of the river, north or south, as our sampan should be about a mile from the entrance to take us on board the launch or Hakka boat to dine and sleep. The next morning can be devoted to such ground as has yielded the best results the previous day, with a trip through Kam-Tin-Ho and the Pat Heung valley, or the Telegraph-pass route, to arrive at Tsin Wan by evening. If this, with the climb, is too much, take the direction to Castle Peak, all nearly level country, and having sent the steam launch and boat round you should meet them about 5 o'clock in the evening.

## PROGRAMME No. 8.

### To Mirs Bay.

Mirs Bay, or more properly Inner Mirs Bay, Tolo Harbour is formed by an arm of the sea entering the land in a south-westerly direction from the outer or Mirs Bay proper. The direct opposite to Deep Bay which is one vast expanse of shallow water, Inner Mirs Bay is approached by a narrow strait about five miles in length leading to a continuation of inlets and narrow channels with deep water in almost every direction. As a place for sport it is limited to ducks and geese with a few snipe and curlew, the villages and hills furnishing pigeons and partridges. Little is attempted at Mirs Bay in the early season and it is generally about China New Year in the months of January and February that much attention is given to the place. As a health resort for a thorough change it is considered good, the scenery and general surroundings differing much from Hongkong, A three or four days or even a week's trip with a party of four or five can be made very enjoyable. Preliminary arrangements should be as follows, having a due regard for the commissariat. Two days before a start is contemplated engage a large sized Hakka boat with a full complement of a crew, and let them set sail early in the morning with all the heavy gear, bedding, provisions, &c., on board, bound for Sha-tin by the outside route which, according to the strength of the monsoon, will take them from 30 or 60 hours. Sometimes it is impossible to get round, *this is not very often.* but then the boat will return in time to let the party know. Having arrived at her destination the boat will prepare for, and await the party by way of the gap at the back of Kowloon. Everything ready, a start should be made in the afternoon of the second or third day, leaving not later than 3 o'clock by steam launch to Kowloon City, thence climb the hill and descend to the vally when you should arrive at the boat by 6 or 6.30 o'clock. There is little to be shot on the way so no time need be wasted.

Having reached the Hakka boat the first thing to do is to engage small boats like punts for the three or four days, according to the length of the trip. These boats should be in attendance the whole time from 5 o'clock in the morning. This being satisfactorily arranged, a wash, a good dinner and a cigar should prepare one for a good night's rest with pleasant anticipations. The next morning rise at 5 o'clock, coffee, &c., &c., and then to the small boats either singly or in couples—the boatmen know exactly where to go.

Mirs Bay contains a number of very pretty inlets many of them completely land locked. Plover Cove is *very* interesting as also Starling Inlet the most northern arm of the bay, approached by crossing the peninsula from the head of a creek on the northern shore of Plover Cove, about one hour's walk.

As suggested before, several days can be pleasantly spent in these waters, it is therefore not necessary to go into further details of the programme. Any likely looking places ashore might be tried especially if dogs are available, as *in season* pheasants are known to haunt the covers all round the bay. The time being up, a return can be made by the outside passage if preferred and the weather is not too rough, otherwise a climb over the hill again is the alterative.

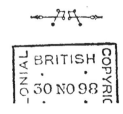

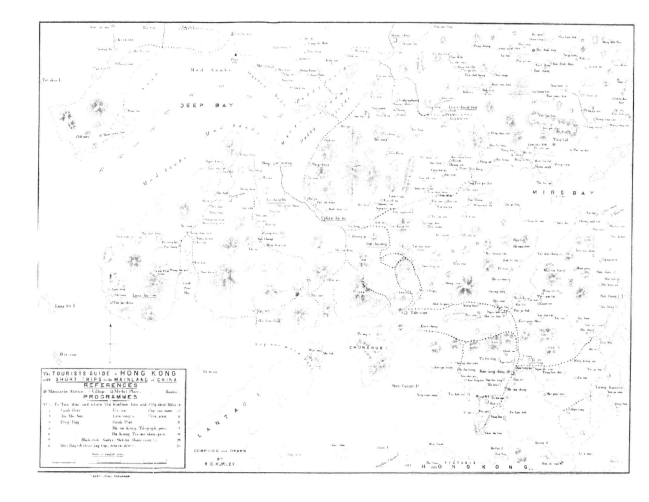

DEEP BAY

MIRS BAY

LANTAU

CHUNCHUEI

HONG KONG

VICTORIA

The **TOURISTS GUIDE** to **HONG KONG**
with **SHORT TRIPS** to the **MAINLAND** of **CHINA**
**REFERENCES**
Ⓜ Mandarin Station    Village    Ⓜ Market Place    Routes

**PROGRAMMES**

No 1. To Tai-o Wan and return via Kowloon City and City about Miles 10
2. Castle Peak          Un-san          Cup-ani-mun    12
3. Tai Mo San          Lam-tong-o      Tin-wan        8
4. Deep Bay            Castle Peak                    8
5.                     Ma-on Kong, Telegraph pass.    5
6.                     Pat-kwong Tea-mo-shan-pass.    16
7. Black-rock  Sankai  Shek-ha, Sham-suen.           20
8. Mirs Bay—A three-day trip, return direct          25

Scale in English miles

COMPILED and DRAWN
BY
R. C. HURLEY.

TRADE        MARK

# H. Price & Co.,

## Wine, Spirit, Ale and Stout Merchants.

LIQUORS of all descriptions kept in Stock.

### SAMPLES & PRICE LISTS ON APPLICATION.

*Sole Agents for :*

Moet and Chandon's Champagne.

Eugene Clicquot's Champagne.

Bouché Fils & Co.'s Champagne.

H. Lenoy & Co.'s Champagne.

Kohler and Van Bergen's American Claret.

Hanappier & Co.'s French Claret.

Langenbach and Sohne's Hock.

Dunville & Co.'s Irish Whisky.

Distillers Co., Ld. Scotch Whisky.

John Dewar & Sons, Ld. Scotch Whisky.

R. B. Hayden's American Whisky.

Gooderham and Wort's Canadian Whisky.

Ind Coope & Co.'s Ale and Stout.

T. B. Hall & Co.'s Ale and Stout.

Jubilee Beer.        A. D. C. Beer.

D. C. L. Gin.

Xeres Vermouth.

Hirano Water,

&c.,    &c.,    &c.

TRIAL ORDERS SOLICITED.

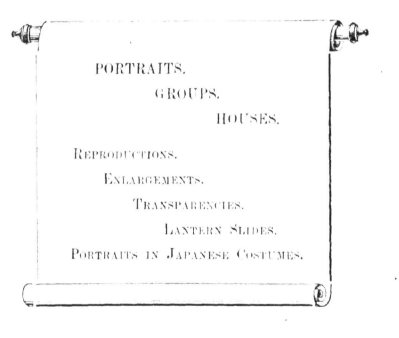

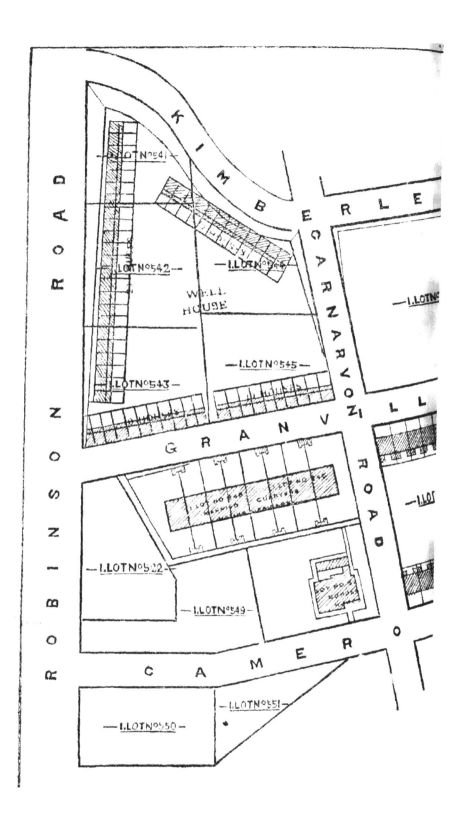

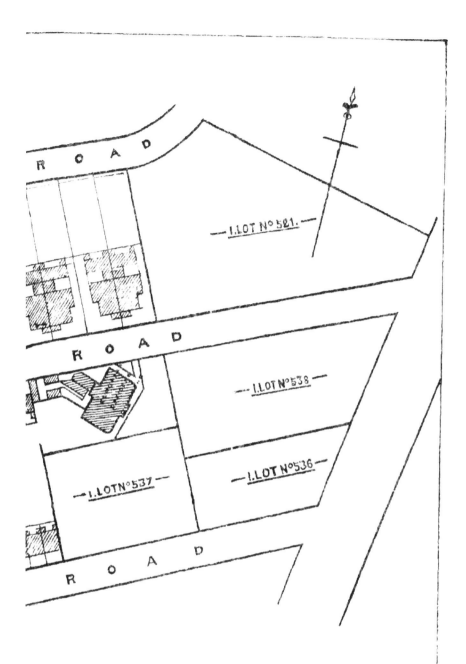

ROAD

I. LOT No 521.

ROAD

I. LOT No 538

I. LOT No 537

I. LOT No 536

ROAD

HUMPHREYS ESTATE & FINANCE Co Lot

SKETCH PLAN OF KOWLOON PROPERTY

SCALE 100 FEET TO 1 INCH

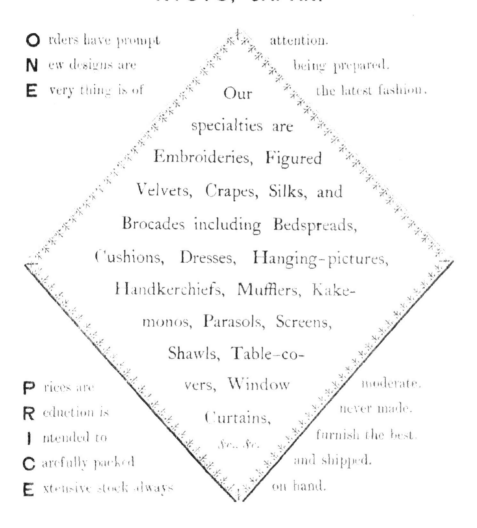

CPSIA information can be obtained
at www.ICGtesting.com
Printed in the USA
BVHW021939290523
665022BV00015B/165